BLACK LAUGHTER

Llewelyn Powys

BLACK LAUGHTER

REDCLIFFE
Bristol

First published in 1924
by Harcourt, Brace & Co.

This edition first published
in 1983 by Redcliffe Press Ltd,
14 Dowry Square, Bristol 8

© *Eve Elwin*

ISBN 0 905459 54 7

Printed in Great Britain by
Villiers Publications Ltd.

BLACK LAUGHTER

INTRODUCTION

*

In the writing on Africa contained in my book *Ebony and Ivory,* the aim was literary and æsthetic rather than personal. The effect I have endeavoured to produce in *Black Laughter* is that of a closer, more intimate reproduction of the casual diurnal occurrences in an alien environment as they impinged upon a receptive nature. Even here, of course, one's instinct for æsthetic effect was bound to play some part in arranging and presenting the given material, but my desire has been to suppress any stylistic quality so that the rank, crude savour of the skin, so to speak, of this sinister continent might present itself to the reader unmitigated by any but the faintest literary effects. However, fortunately for all of us, past experiences, bitter though they may have been, have a way of losing much of their anguish when viewed in retrospection. A certain glow of romance, one of time's happiest legacies, gathers about our more fortunate memories, while the rest tend to be forgotten. For obvious reasons it has been impossible for me to be more explicit with regard to the personalities and places to

which reference is made. This volume contains
in the identical form in which they were written
certain stories which have already appeared in
the New York *Evening Post*, and my thanks are
due to the editors of that paper for allowing
them to be republished here. The account of my
friend Merishu's death appeared some time ago
in *The Freeman*.

LLEWELYN POWYS

CONTENTS

CHAPTER ONE
Chequered Shadows

*

It was nearly midnight and the small Uganda train, which for a day and a half had been dragging itself across the vast highland plateau of East Africa, was approaching the station that for five years was to represent my link with the civilized world. There being no coal in the country, the fires of the locomotive were fed by wood, and as I sat at the window of the diminutive darkened carriage I watched the sparks from the engine flicker past me into the velvet African darkness. Some of these illumined fragments passed out of sight still undimmed; some floated upwards, some downwards, and as I followed with my eyes their erratic movements my excited thoughts became charged with many strange apprehensions.

These sprightly morsels of living fire, dancing with such eager futility against the mysterious depths of that obscure midnight, mixed themselves curiously with the conception of life which had been gradually forming in my mind. Nations and individuals were like that . . . they sprang

13

into existence, they flickered, they fell back into oblivion, only the dark reality behind remaining unknown and illimitable. Indeed, it was probable that the intelligences of half of the human race, privileged to be afoot on the earth during that momentous September of the year 1914, were troubled by a similar sense of foreboding, of insecurity. The distant echoes of the guns that I had heard as the Union Castle liner left the Port of London had set a sombre and bewildering vibration agog in the craniums of white, black, and yellow alike. And while my own race, along with the others, was causing the very crust of the planet to tremble with its barbaric and malignant onslaughts, here was I being tossed by an indifferent and casual destiny into the heart of the one continent which remained unexplored, and, indeed, only half waked from the dangerous somnolence of its primitive condition.

The train came to a standstill. I had arrived at my destination. I saw lights and what appeared to be a station shanty dimly visible behind half-a-dozen newly grown trees. I dragged my luggage out of the carriage and waited by the side of the track. There were a few cries in an unknown language and then the lumbering vans continued on their way towards the Great Lake.

I had expected my brother Willie to meet me, and, seeing a human figure near the shanty, I walked towards it. It was the Indian station-master. He told me in broken English that he had seen nothing of my brother. He then conducted me to a square wooden shed a hundred yards away where he informed me I could sleep. It had been built for benighted settlers – a flimsy erection of match-boarding roofed with sheets of corrugated iron. It contained a cheap bedstead in one corner, but the rest, except for a lantern, was unfurnished. When the man had gone I put out the light, and with my great-coat still over me, lay down. I left the door open so that I could look out into the cavernous blackness of Africa. For some time I was too excited to sleep. I could see nothing and yet during those tense hours in that little room the weight and vastness of this alien environment outside pressed in upon my consciousness. Well I knew that this particular oblong ebony-black aperture opposite opened out upon no honeysuckle lanes, no dreaming orchards, no secluded terraces, such as had surrounded me since childhood, but, instead, miles

15

and thousands of miles of wild grassy lands, broken now by enormous glacial mountains, now by stagnant lakes, now by overgrown forests, and inhabited by no simple labourers of Saxon origin, but by naked black men, asleep at that moment by the white ashes of a myriad camp-fires with their tall spears ready to hand.

At last I dozed, but it was not for long. Suddenly I found myself sitting bolt up on the creaking wires of the bed. Certainly I had heard something. I listened. There was surely nothing to startle my subconscious self in the constant insect-murmur that came in from outside. Was it merely a fancy, a nightmare, such as I would experience sometimes sleeping out on a summer night in the garden at home, when, mingled with my dreams, would come the sharp witch-bark of a fox moving along under the uneven shadows of a cool hayfield hedge? I could not tell. I waited. And then I heard it again. This time there could be no mistake – a dull, heavy reverberation, like distant thunder, which rose and fell and died away into a sigh. Remote as the sound undoubtedly was, its force and volume were so great that one felt the hollow vaulted night retained its vibration long after the actual roaring had subsided. And what a menace there had been in it! Sitting there on that rusty bed I felt my body alert with a hundred ancient ancestral misgivings such as in far-off days must have disturbed our fathers, the first progenitors of men, when denuded of claws, denuded of horns, denuded of fangs, they yet had the audacity to challenge the sovereignty of the wild beasts. With the utmost expedition I got up and closed the door. Even so I found it quite impossible to sleep. I kept listening and listening for that sound to be repeated. I had not to wait long; and now it seemed to me much nearer. I was seized with panic. I realized for the first time the inestimable advantage of living behind stone and brick. For half-an-hour the sound was repeated at short intervals and every time its guttural growlings grew louder. Obviously the lion was proceeding in the direction of the station, and as the moments advanced my confidence in the flimsy wooden shed which sheltered me steadily declined. I remembered having been told that lions practically never broke into a human habitation. The chances against such procedure were, I had been assured, one in a thousand. As each minute elapsed I became more

17

stubbornly convinced that it was to be my ill
fate to become myself an example of this unfortunate exception. I felt like a mouse, a little
nervous grey mouse, shut up in a box-trap which
an enormous tabby-cat had spied and was slowly
and deliberately advancing towards. Presently I
actually heard the lion moving about like a cow
or horse. *I could hear it breathing.* I sat motionless and silent lest I should attract attention. I
wondered why on earth I had ever come to such
a country and from the bottom of my heart
wished East Africa to the devil.

At last everything became once more silent.
Slowly the hours passed until I realized that it
was growing light. I went to the door, opened
it, and suspiciously looked out. Except for the
narrow-gauged railroad tracks and a wide expanse of dusty brown grass there was nothing to
be seen. I stepped out and walked across to the
station. The Indian official, with a little round
turban-like cap on his head, was looking out of
a narrow window. I asked him whether he had
heard the lion. 'Yes,' he said, 'I heard him; he
come every night, he a polite lion, he no hurt
anyone, he drink water from tanky.' It was perfectly true. From where I stood I could see a

18

pool of water gleaming in the slanting sunlight.
It was filled by the overflow of a huge iron tank
which stood by the track and had evidently been
put there to serve as a reservoir for the engines.
I went across to inspect the place. The pool lay
at the foot of a small embankment, and I saw
where the animal had stood to slake its thirst.
In all directions the damp ground at the edge of
the water had received the impression of enormous pads. I had been used enough to seeing the
hoof-marks of cattle and horses, the footprints of
dogs, or of an occasional badger, but these great,
round, flat indentures gave me a very odd sensation as I glanced down at them.

The sun was now well up on the horizon, and
as I sat under a wattle-tree sipping a cup of hot
tea which the Indian provided, I let my eyes roam
over the immediate vicinity. I discovered that
there were other habitations besides the station-
house – a group of low huts, some hundred yards
away, belonging to more Asiatics. I could see
them opening up their corrugated shutters to the
inquisitive gaze of half-a-dozen natives who,
dressed in European rags, were standing about
with an air of impertinent nonchalance.

Beyond this African vignette, which had

already taken upon itself that shadowless clear-cut appearance that belongs to the tropics, was a rough roadway leading off into a mass of low scrub. At the edge of this bushy country grew three or four tremendous cactus-trees which gave to the landscape a most grotesque look. They might have been sentinels – sentinels with a thousand flat-palmed hands, placed there to expostulate with Europeans and warn them of the deadly perils that the land concealed. In after years these particular trees, whenever I passed them, never failed to revive in me the mood of that morning; their abnormal verdure and scaly, python-like trunks suggesting in themselves an anguished origin completely remote from that sense of calm and aloofness which one associates with the high, still columns of English trees.

It was, however, over the round chequered shadows cast by these very African growths that the familiar figure of my brother a few minutes later suddenly appeared.

CHAPTER TWO

From the Gibbet-Tree

*

My brother at this time was managing an agricultural farm in the highlands leading to Laikipia. He lived in a small stone house which had been built by an Indian mason. The veranda in front overlooked two hundred acres of ploughed land, which grew peas, potatoes, flax, and barley. This diminutive farm was enclosed on one side by the rough scrub country of the ordinary veldt, and on the other by a forest which stretched away at the foot of a tall escarpment as far as eye could see. It was a surprise to come suddenly upon this oasis of cultivation in the midst of a country which still remained virginal.

Towards evening, when the mists of the light rains drove across the peas and potatoes, or hung about the brown cone-shaped flax-stacks, the prospect would take upon itself a strangely familiar appearance; but, coincident with such reassuring impressions, would come others, impressions curiously disturbing in their suggestion of forces inimical to man's purpose. One had but to step out of the little garden of geraniums, which my brother had arranged and planted round the house, to find oneself in the actual jungle, in dark, overgrown places which for thousands of years had remained undisturbed. It was this abrupt juxtaposition of the tamed with the untamed, at one's very doorstep, so to speak, which affected the nerves with an ever-present feeling of insecurity. One felt that oneself and one's handful of black servants were permitted a foothold here on sufferance only – that in a moment of time, for a mere whim, these stately, wicked, bearded cedar-trees might conspire with their long-clawed parasitical creepers to obliterate one's handiwork and reassert their ancient domination. Indeed, I was conscious of this feeling every single hour of my stay on that upland farm. I came to realize what it was to live in a place where nature was in the ascendancy.

I would sit in a shaded corner of the veranda watching the humming-birds flitting about the petals of the coloured flowers which in all directions expanded so passionately in the hard tropical sunlight, and then I would suddenly become aware that I was being looked at, that from behind the trellis, or from behind the bloom of a mammoth nasturtium, a haggard and very old chameleon was peering at me intelligently, cynically. At night it would be even worse. Then, when the flat Equatorial moon would blandly illuminate this unregenerate section of the earth's surface, the soul of Africa would become articulate. Hyenas would moan as they slunk along the darkened banks of the forest streams nosing for death with heavy, obtuse jowls. Leopards would cause the pale trunks of the forest trees to echo and re-echo with the sound of their calling. Jackals in an ecstasy of crafty expectation would go yelping across the open veldt. From every festooned branch of the forest the hyraxes would cry and croon to one another, while from tiny crevices in the bark of each piece of ancient timber the African crickets would grow strangely vocal. Often at night when we went out to draw water from the rain-tank at the back of the house we could hardly hear each other speak, so audible had the great continent become, that continent which all day long lies in a dull sleep under the hypnotic rays of an evil sun, only to grow in the high noon of midnight so wild, so merciless, so alarmingly voluble.

Every morning I used to spend an hour or two learning the Swahili language from my Kikuyu servant, Kamoha. He was an extremely intelligent boy and till the day I left Africa was my constant companion. In the afternoons I would accompany my brother on shooting expeditions. We would cross the mountain stream which separated us from the forest, a stream which harboured no fish, but whose waters ran eddying through black sunken pools over a bed of iron volcanic rock. At regular intervals along its edge the density of the forest was broken by narrow, well-trodden game-paths leading down to this or that water-hole – water-holes that by day and night received a hundred thirsty jowls, a hundred thirsty muzzles, a hundred thirsty snouts. At each of these places, if one looked for them, one could see silver-white bones, witnessing to the innumerable animal tragedies that had been enacted at these terrible death-traps. Sometimes the damp mud near the water would be marked with pointed hoofs, sometimes with the long-toed footprints of monkeys, and sometimes with the round heavy spoor of a carnivore. We would follow one of these paths into the depths of the forest. On each side of us the soft leaf-mould would be cloaked with masses of maiden-hair fern. My brother would be on the look-out for bushbuck, and when one of these tough, lusty little animals fell after the report of his rifle what a clamour would arise! The green parrots would scream, the colobus monkeys would leap with chattering expostulations from branch to branch, and great white-winged turkey-birds would circle above the tops of the trees.

And then we would begin to scale the escarpment, mounting higher and ever higher up the slippery root-covered path to find ourselves at last once more in daylight. Standing there on the summit of the escarpment what a view would be presented to our eyes – miles upon miles of open, rolling country, broken by green-bordered rivers, by the demon-haunted, rush-grown stretches of Lake El Bordossat stretching away to the distant slopes of the Aberdare Mountains lying swart in the afternoon sun!

Often and often I have sat there on the cliff's edge and seen zebra, kongoni, ostriches moving across the yellow plains below. Occasionally I would make out the black unmistakable tub-like form of a rhinoceros advancing slowly, soberly towards some verdant refuge. I found a sheltered ledge where I would sit for hours surveying that stupendous scene. I marked the place by a dead olive-tree, whose naked, crooked arms held on their topmost branches three round ant-nests which had the appearance and size of human skulls. I could see this gibbet-tree from a distance of several hundred yards, and when once safely ensconced the wild life of the place would continue as though I was not there. The klip-springers would bound from rock to rock, or with delicate legs rigid, stand poised and expectant. The rock-rabbits would scuttle from fissure to fissure. The eagles and white-breasted hawks would sweep fiercely through the clear air uttering strange intractable cries. And as I viewed these unfamiliar aspects of life, so different from the sheep meadows, the cattle pastures, the thatched grange scenery of my home, over which in autumn the ragged-winged rooks would circle, it would seem to me as though I had been permitted by the intervention of some extraordinary magic to contemplate the round earth as it must have appeared when first it was moulded and set spinning.

And then as the round sun dropped towards the horizon I would hurry back, anxious to be through the belt of forest before dark. It was on one of these occasions as my brother and I hastened through some tall red grass that I tripped and fell. I had put my foot into a round hole sunk some six inches into the ground. An elephant had passed this way on its yearly migration to the bamboo forests during the wet season, and at each step the enormous animal had taken there had been left in the soggy drenched ground a diminutive pit. Presently we came upon other similar tracks, with large heaps of dry dung scattered here and there, dung dropped doubtless six months before when some of these bulky, placid, sage creatures had passed over the escarpment on their familiar journey.

Once through the forest and across the river we felt ourselves, with a feeling of relief, back once more in an environment upon which human beings had at least made some impression. There was a stir of human life. The black women were carrying water up from the river. There was the sound of native talk, of native laughter, and the air was tainted with the smoke of fires filtering up through the thatch of the round huts and rising like dedicated incense into the hollow firmament above, already tremulous and quivering with the indefinable murmurs of the on-coming night.

27

CHAPTER THREE
Wild Elephants

*

MY brother had an indiscriminate pack of dogs of various breeds which he used for hunting leopards, cheetahs, hyenas, jackals, wart-hogs, porcupines, and serval cats. There was a large mongrel, a pointer called 'Ugonjwa,' an Airedale called 'Mac,' another called 'Pat,' two or three more whose names I have forgotten, and 'Micky,' a plucky wire-haired terrier.

We used to go hunting on Sunday mornings, my brother on foot and I, thanks to his generosity, on his kicking mule. We would try to get away before daybreak. I remember the first time I went out with him we put the dogs into a large patch of nettles some hundred yards wide. These African nettles are to be avoided, as their sting is far more serious than that of the European variety. However, hardly had we taken up a position overlooking the place than we heard the pack beginning to give tongue, and became aware of a considerable movement not far from the ant-hill upon which we were waiting. It was an exciting moment. I half expected to see a lion or a leopard break cover, so great was the commotion. In reality it turned out to be three cheetahs.

Like a flash they darted off in the direction of some scrub about a mile or so to the right. Away we went after them, dogs and all. The two leading cheetahs after a while turned and made for a river-bed. The third, which was the largest, evidently felt himself too hard pressed to attempt the farther distance. He kept on in the direction of the scrub. The dogs were close behind him when he entered and a few moments later, by the sound of their baying, we knew that they had treed him. We reached the place. There, high up in an olive-tree, was the animal, looking immense as it lay with its spotted belly close along one of the boughs. As soon as we appeared it lost all interest in the dogs and turned its head in our direction, snarling vindictively. No lion could have made an uglier face. My brother sent a bullet through its shoulder and it dropped to the ground – a golden ball – to be instantly covered by the eager pack. Before it was skinned I examined it closely. I remember being surprised by the number of ticks it carried. It was the first large carnivorous

animal I had seen dead and its lovely pelt
sheltered great numbers of these loathsome
parasites. Its head was not quite as large as a
leopard's and its shoulders and paws not nearly
so heavy. On the back of its neck it had a
curious ruff of long hair.

After serval cats, wart-hogs were our most
usual quarry. These hideous, heavily tusked pigs
would set off over the veldt at a fine pace with
their tails held erect. Whenever they saw fit to
go to earth in one of the disused ant-bear holes
which serve them as homes they would always
swing sharply round so as to enter the aperture
backwards. It was quaint to see them do this.
One speculates as to the number of severe
lessons given to wart-hogs before they came to
understand that to go down holes head first put
the most undefended portion of their bodies at
a grave disadvantage. A wart-hog standing at
the mouth of its hole presents a really imposing
front, its great tusks white against the earth, its
head held in readiness for a swift sally, should
one of the dogs come within reach. On such
occasions we could sometimes make them bolt
by stamping upon the ground above them. If
they did, they would come out with a rush and

a cloud of dust and be a hundred yards away before we had realized what had happened. Natives declare that lions, if they are very hungry, will have resort to this stamping trick and catch the pigs as they emerge. I myself am sceptical about the truth of this. It seems to me a practice a little too tricky for an animal which is so proud in its eating that it won't even trouble to kill sheep. I must confess, however, that I did on one occasion see the remains of a wart-hog obviously killed by a lion just outside its hole and the marks of a lion's paw all round, just as if it actually had been giving the ground one or two good thumps.

Micky, the small terrier, and Ugonjwa, the pointer, got me into a nasty scrape one afternoon soon after my arrival. My brother had gone off on the mule to try to find the camp of some Somali traders who were said to have brought down from the north a fine herd of Boran cattle. I was alone, with nothing much to do, and the fancy took me to go into the forest to see if I could not shoot a bushbuck. I have always been an incredibly bad shot and perhaps for this very reason I was especially tickled by the idea of showing my brother a trophy upon his return. I

31

knew he sometimes took Micky into the forest, as this little dog was more obedient than the others, and I let out Ugonjwa also, because I had taken rather a fancy to this great flat-browed pointer whose eyes had so tender and meditative a look.

I crossed the river and entered the forest by a small path along which I had often been with my brother. I advanced cautiously. Once or twice I heard some animal crash away through the undergrowth, but I never got a chance to shoot. The game-path down which I went gave out a curious damp smell like decaying laurel bushes and the branches against which I brushed were chill and cold, their leaves like the limp and horribly thin hands of a dead man. Presently the path came to an end in a mass of foliage through which it was quite impossible to pass. I sat down with my gun on my knee. The only trace of any animal I could see was a hard dry fragment of lime-like hyena's dung. Micky had gone forward; but the pointer settled himself at my side and began biting at a patch of mange on his back which was still yellow from the preparation of mustard and oil which my brother had rubbed on it that morning.

Suddenly, without the least warning, the whole forest was echoing with the most awful noise that I had ever heard. It was like the screeching whistle of a railway train blowing full blast. It was deafening, bewildering. I was on my feet in an instant. Forgetting about my gun, I began rushing back along the path up which I had come. I had taken only a few steps when right in front of me, framed in the green forest foliage, I saw the head of an elephant. The animal's trunk was waving backwards and forwards among the branches, its black ears were spread out from its head like great flapping fans, and it was emitting all the time a succession of shrill blasts. I wish I could convey to you how large that head looked. A single glimpse of it was enough for me. I turned and fled. I had hardly reached the place where I had been sitting when I caught sight of the back of another elephant. I dodged again and flung myself desperately through the tangled growths. I came upon a tree which had ropes of heavy creepers reaching from its branches to the ground. I seized some of these with my hands and began pulling myself up, but each time I put any weight on them they gave, and I found myself once more on the

B

ground. During those few seconds I experienced a nightmare sensation such as I shall never forget. There was a crash behind me, and again I dived away on the look-out for some tree whose trunk I could climb. At last I found one and began half swarming and half pulling myself up. I was only just in time. One of the elephants had evidently got wind of me, for it came crashing forward to the very tree up which I was. I remained perfectly still, clinging like a frightened monkey to a branch which I believed to be out of harm's way. I could not see what was happening below, but I felt the cedar sway backwards and forwards as the great beast put its shoulder to it. I felt sick in the stomach. There was an odd fungus on the branch and I concentrated my eyes upon its poisonous colour, wondering whether the next moment I should be shaken out of my position like a ripe medlar. I knew that it is no joke to fall into the power of an infuriated elephant. They simply kneel on you and crush you flat, cracking your ribs as if you were made of wicker-work.

I allowed a full hour to elapse before I began to contemplate a descent from my position. I had heard the sound of the animals growing more and more distant, with Micky still at their heels, but even so I felt very definite misgivings at the thought of finding myself once more on the forest floor. There seemed to me danger at every turn. I suspected appalling ambushes. No gazelle yearling could have been more full of neurotic fears than I was as I tiptoed back to retrieve my gun and with the utmost rapidity got myself out of the forest. Henceforth I resolved to give elephants the widest possible berth, and as far as it was possible for me to do so I kept my resolution.

My brother got back at dusk, and as we sat over our supper of cold venison I recounted my adventure. Happy hours those were, with the sense of security after danger – the stone walls of the little room decorated with horns and skins, and a crackling wood fire on the hearth! Our Kikuyu *mtoto* came in with more logs, and as he bent down to stack the wood by the chimney I remember looking at his round coal-black head and wondering how his ancestors had ever survived to beget him in a country where one encountered elephants within a few yards of one's back door. Ten o'clock found us in our beds on the veranda, but several hours had passed before

I got to sleep. That monstrous shrieking still rang in my ears, giving an uneasy background to all my half-dreams. Outside in the darkness beyond the geraniums, beyond the flimsy wire fence put up to keep out the buck, the muttering African midnight spread itself abroad over the abrupt rocky escarpment, over the treacherous forest, over the naked, shelterless veldt, and above it all, calm, aloof, passionless, shone the constellations, many of which were the same I had looked upon from my bedroom window at home, hanging in an unclouded firmament, far up above the King William pear-tree and the stable roof.

CHAPTER FOUR
A Kikuyu Riot
*

THE early mornings on that forest farm were wonderful. At six o'clock, just as the sun rose, Kamoha would bring us cups of tea, and then we would go out together to an open space in front of the great roughly built barn where the natives gathered each morning to receive directions as to the day's work. Sometimes we employed as many as sixty half-naked Kikuyus, not counting the regular staff of Kavirondos and Swahilis. The boys emerged from their round close huts like so many erect hairless apes. During the rainy season it would often take some time for the sun to break through the clouds. Heavy veils of cold mist would come floating up from the river, and then as we walked along the muddy roadway, washed into deep furrows by the rain of the night before, the whole landscape would suddenly become radiant. The crinkled, dark green, heavily drenched potato leaves would sparkle, flocks of purple scintillating starlings would flash by, and the sedate secretary-birds, as they paced in stately fashion

37

over the stubble, would gleam in the clear fresh light.

We would set the boys in rows pulling flax; and there they would squat, these dusky merry-andrews, chanting strange snatches of Bantu music, with their round skulls hardly higher than the forest of slim stalks. Presently the drivers would bring their oxen down the road for the day's ploughing; Maniki, the Wakamba, whose tribe still followed the ancient cannibal custom of filing the front teeth till they were sharp as needles; Abdulla, the Swahili, whose head was as full of ancient African mythology as a coconut is of milk. They would run by the side of their yoked teams cracking their long whips, and the grotesque hump-backed beasts would hurry forward, their hoofs sliding in the soft mud.

We would then walk back to our house and eat the breakfast of porridge and eggs which Kamoha had prepared, and the little plum-coloured tit-like birds would settle in the rose-bush which climed up the veranda trellis, and butterflies of incredible magnitude and incredible shape would pass from flower to flower, and the steaming air would become charged with

38

alien smells at once enervating and exciting. On such occasions it would seem to me in my simplicity that no continent could be more beautiful, more admirable, than Africa.

Each hour during those first months had its peculiar charm. It was pleasant at midday to sit in the cool near the river and watch the native swineherd bring the pigs down to the water-hole to drink. It was pleasant to wander home through the lilishwa bushes carelessly plucking at their pointed leaves, many of them covered with a down as soft as the tail feathers of a marabou stork. I recall my delight at finding a scabious coming up in that dry alien grass. It seemed extraordinary that this honey-scented flower, so familiar to me on the brambly bracken-covered slopes of the hills of Somerset, should be equally at home in so remote a country. A duiker would be disturbed and go bounding away over the tufted grass, and we would arrive at our house to find some new matter to be dealt with, perhaps a group of raw natives looking for work, natives with painted hair and leather clay-stained wallets and horns full of snuff. Or an old woman would be at the door, the mother of one of the boys, asking for medicine, an interminable

stream of incomprehensible negroid syllables
issuing from her mouth, and with her brown
paps hanging down like withered pears.

At three o'clock the boys knocked off work
and returned up the road singing. It was then
that we would start off on some exploring walk,
passing through places of appalling loneliness,
places fit only as a background for the drowsy,
thoughtless existence of the rhinoceros. We actually came upon the skeleton of one of these
creatures in a certain deserted valley – a huge
heap of white bones! I picked up a great grinder
tooth, with scraps of blackened vegetation still
sticking in its ivory crevices, vegetation that had
been drawn into that indefatigable maw how
long ago!

One afternoon my brother shot a waterbuck in
a distant forest. The animal was wounded only,
and he and Abdulla left me and rushed after it.
I waited several hours for his return. Eventually
I decided he must have gone back some other
way and turned to go home. It began to rain,
rain black African rain, and I stumbled on
through that torrential downpour full of melancholy misgivings. Once I heard behind me the
long, low dismal cry of a wild hunting dog. It

was dark before I smelt the reassuring tang of the camp-fires and came in to find hot water waiting for me. But even dry clothes could not relieve my uneasiness. I kept looking out into the darkness, hoping for some sign of my brother's return. The night seemed lowering and more than sinister. It was as though some treacherous enemy that one had for a long time suspected suddenly stood revealed in all his malignity. The mere thought of that deserted spot in the forest where we had parted filled my mind with ugly half-formulated fears. What was it like there now, near that fallen giant tree whose sides had been blackened by a hundred bush-fires? Surely the very raindrops must feel fear as they coursed their way down its bole, down its charred bole, the surface of which showed clearly where leopards had recently sharpened their claws. And then came a sound outside, the cry ' *Bwana nakuja!* ' from Komoha; and there he was, drenched to the skin, with the head and hide of the waterbuck over his arm, and Abdulla behind, with great haunches of venison suspended from a stick.

I soon learnt enough Swahili to be able to speak to the natives. On the few occasions, there-

fore, that my brother left the farm I undertook
to superintend the work. It did not take me
long to discover that this business of organizing
the labour of a hundred raw Africans was
by no means as easy as it looked. I very
well remember the first ugly experience that I
had.

The boys on the farm for several weeks had
been clamouring for meat, and my brother
decided to give them an old ox that was too lame
to work. As he was going to be away that day
he asked me to do the shooting and butchering
of the animal. At about three in the afternoon,
when the work on the shamba was over, I had
the doomed animal led out to an open place
near the boys' huts and shot it there. The very
moment it fell I realized I was in for a difficult
time. The sound of the shot brought the natives
out like so many hyenas. They crowded round
the carcass as though they wanted to tear it to
pieces with their own hands. I tried to keep
them back, but as half of them did not know
Swahili, I found difficulty in making them
understand that I merely wanted room for the
skinning and cutting up of the beast. As the
half-dozen Swahilis who worked on the farm

were more civilized than the Kikuyus, I commandeered them for the work. Meanwhile the riff-raff remained standing a little way off. When the meat had been divided into joints and lay in heaps on the grass I made as just a distribution as I possibly could. For some reason the Kikuyus got into their heads that they were not being given their proper share. When I tried to explain they simply jabbered at me. Presently they began to sulk, and swore they did not want any at all. I was sick and tired of the whole business, and in a fit of irritation took them at their word and portioned out the meat amongst the Swahilis and Kavirondos. As soon as the Kikuyus realized what I was doing, a great hubbub arose, especially when they saw, with their own eyes, the meat being carried away into the other boys' huts. One of them, a huge naked negro, evidently the ringleader, began chanting some gibberish, while the rest, sitting round on their haunches, banged at the ground with their clubs and short native swords. I inquired from the Swahilis the meaning of this demonstration, and as well as I could understand they told me that they were praying God that everyone who partook of the meat should be poisoned. This did not sound very serious, so I presently departed, glad enough to escape from the noise and clamour.

I had hardly got inside our house when I heard the sound of the Kikuyu war-cry: *'Uwee! Uwee! Uwee!'* At the same instant Kamoha came flying in to say that the Kikuyus were murdering the Swahilis. Snatching up a rifle I ran back in the direction of the huts.

I found a veritable battle in progress, clubs and swords flying in all directions; one Swahili already on the ground, another with blood streaming from a gash in his crown. It struck me that I might quiet the mêlée by shooting over their heads. Apparently the Kikuyus considered this a sign that I had definitely taken sides against them, for they all with one accord came surging towards me. I got my back against one of the huts and covered them as best I could with my rifle. Whether to shoot or not I could not tell. It was an extraordinarily tense moment, and I shall not forget my sensations, with those hideous physiognomies yapping and grimacing at me. I really do not know how it would have ended if my brother at that moment had not appeared on the scene.

Just as he reached our house he had heard the

report of the gun, and guessing that there was something wrong had galloped his mule up to the huts. He dismounted and came strolling up to the place where I was standing. His general air of coolness changed the situation at once. *'Mzungu!'* ('White man!') the Kikuyus cried and gave way. He asked them in their own language what they thought they were doing, swore at them roundly, calling them the sons of bastard-snakes, and then, treating them as if they were a lot of naughty children, sent them back to their houses. Only the big leader looked as if he might make further trouble. He came up to my brother with the utmost truculence, brandishing a long spear. In a moment a well-directed blow from my brother's fist had sent him toppling backwards. There was no hesitation with the others after that. They went off immediately, full of chatter about *Bwana Poli Poli,* or the Slow Master, who, they declared, was never afraid, never lost his temper, and was stronger than a black-maned lion. If the incident gave the natives much to talk about, it certainly gave me food for much useful thinking.

CHAPTER FIVE
The Rhythm of Africa

*

WE would often go out hunting porcupine. After supper we would collect a number of boys, let out the dogs, and with spears in our hands make our way towards the potato patch. Porcupine used to do an astounding amount of damage to these vegetables. They would work right through the rows, unburying the roots. They came from great distances for the satisfaction of doing this. We sometimes hunted them back to holes in a rocky hill-side several miles away. They had a kind of small rattle of quills on the ends of their tails, and when once we had started one of them out of the potatoes it would make a most infernal jingling with this instrument as it trundled along over the veldt. Hunting porcupine requires no little skill. They have a trick of dashing off at top speed and then, at the most exciting moment of the hunt, stopping dead still and rushing backwards, reversing gear, so to speak, to the utter confusion of their pursuers, who, unless very alert, find themselves in collision with a curious battering-ram of sharp spikes.

Most of the dogs, from bitter experience, gave chase to these animals in a very wary and diffident way, keeping always at a safe distance. Micky we never took with us on these occasions, because we knew that nothing would keep him back when once his blood was up. The rest of the pack knew just what to do. They would run the porcupine until it was out of breath and then bay it up till we and the boys appeared. We used to have some exciting moments even then. The light shed by our lantern was never sufficient, and the fretful animal would charge backwards and forwards in all directions, its tail keeping up a continuous jangling like a bunch of keys at an old woman's apron. I have known the leg of a boy to be speared right through by a porcupine. When the animal was dead we used to pull out the best quills, and my brother would send them home, wrapped up in *The East African Standard,* to be used as pen-holders. The carcass we would leave where it was, that extraordinary carcass, with its strong legs and black rabbit-like face. If we happened to pass by the place during the next few days the air to windward would be villainously tainted, but this would not last long; very soon the carrion birds,

47

the hyenas, the jackals, the rats, the ants, would clear it all up, so that, except for a little heap of black-and-white quills, nothing would remain of the odd bulky animal which possessed so keen a relish for the imported American root and knew how to find its way about over the veldt on the darkest night. Kill! Kill! Kill! that was what one had to do to keep in tune with the African rhythm, with that inexorable rhythm, the sublimest cadence of which is only to be heard when backbones are being snapped and throats cut.

After all, men must live; and when an army of black ants streamed into the house to devour a shoulder of mutton, what else was one to do but pour boiling water on their crowded roadway, that roadway which stretched up the stone wall and over the window sill. In Africa not only is Nature indifferent to the fate of the manifold forms of life she has created, she is malignant also. In all directions a crafty and merciless war is being waged. It was not nice for the porcupine to be stabbed to death nor for the ants to be boiled alive, but neither was it nice for 'Ugonjwa's' newly born puppies to have their blind eyes eaten out of their heads by these same insects.

It is in accord with cosmic laws that the contraction of a planet should cause the death of three hundred thousand human beings. The thing is done blindly, accidentally; but look more narrowly at the picture, as it is possible to do in Africa, and it will be seen that on the very planet's crust a sly contest is being waged, deliberately, consciously, and without quarter, hand against hide, claw against horn, and beak against fur. Kill! Kill! Kill! that is the mandate of Africa, and the more assiduously it is obeyed the more in harmony one becomes with that Equatorial environment where the motive principles of nature lie stark and undisguised. I was not slow to learn this simple law. To stay one's hand would mean death; 'twere best to strike with a free heart.

Leopards used to give us a great deal of trouble on that forest farm. They would sometimes enter the shed, squeezing themselves through some unnoticed opening to carry off a pig. We would set gun-traps for them down by the water-hole. We baited these ingenious contrivances with dead animals – a dead goat, perhaps. We built a protection of thorns round the carcass and tied it by a string to a trigger-stick which was adjusted so as to discharge the gun (set horizontally a foot above the ground) at the slightest movement. We used to set the trap just before the sun went down. Prior to making the final adjustments, however, we would drag the bait along all the neighbouring paths, so that the leopard might be directed by its smell to the trap. This occupation was usually reserved for me, and many a curious emotion I used to experience as I pulled the lifeless weight over roots and tussocks till it was disfigured with dust. Meanwhile, my brother would be working away at the thorn protection in some bushes under a group of cedar-trees.

And then darkness would fall and the air would become full of unexplained noises and strange unexpected smells, and the African wind would blow against our faces and set the long tufted branches of the forest trees tossing against each other, and we would stumble through the grass to the old familiar shamba-track and so come nearer and nearer to the small lamp-lit house, where there would be boys to be seen, and labour-tickets to be marked, and, perhaps, a letter to write on the cheap thin paper we used to get from the Indian shopman at the station.

Then when Kamoha had cleared supper away we would sit over a crackling wood fire and talk of old days in Somersetshire, talk of the long walks we had taken together down by the River Yeo in midsummer, when the hayfields were still uncut and the grazing meadows at three in the afternoon would be alive with sun-burnt boys with flowers in their caps, and with white bonneted girls, and with peaceful mild-eyed red cows who kept lazily switching the horseflies away with their heavy matted tails. How mellow, how immemorial it used to look, the group of docile animals, the bowed human backs, the tall milk-pails standing silver-white amid the nettles and umbelliferous flowers under the shadow of the hedgerow elms. We would recall also the Christmas holidays, the occasion when we would take our skates out of the schoolroom cupboard and polish them with sandpaper against the next day when we would go to Pit Pond over the crisp frozen fields, the very molehills of which were so hard that no amount of kicking would make any impression on their frost-gripped surfaces.

Suddenly, clear and unmistakable out of the darkness, would come the heavy booming of a

gun. I never heard one of those gun-traps go
off without a curious shock. One felt as though
oneself was present down there under the trees
by the black flowing water in utter loneliness.
Had the bullet done its work, one wondered, or
was the animal at that very moment plunging
back into the forest unharmed?

Morning would come at last, and we would
put on our heavy boots and khaki trousers and
set off through the damp scrub down to the trap,
and looking over the crest of the hill, there
before us, stretched out upon the cool, shining,
dewy grass, would lie the long snake-like body
of a gilded ebon-spotted cat. The mere fact that
such an animal should actually be abroad upon
the earth used to seem to me amazing, yet in
the fecundity of this land all the animals of
creation, it would seem, were brought to birth.
There by the water-hole, with the sunlight
slanting across the tops of the forest trees, we
would take out our knives – our 'Bushman's
Friends' – and set to work at skinning our
trophy. Far above us in the branches were the
colobus monkeys, agile arboreals in white-and-
black jackets, filling the greedy pouches of their
cheeks with the tiny green berries they love. It

was a laborious task, this affair of separating with deft slits the decorated pelt from the sinewy body, and how red, how sinister the body looked when it was naked! What taut muscles! What a suggestion of lithe and dangerous strength knit together with elastic ligaments! And how heavy that limp skin was, that limp gorgeous skin that smelt of the fierce leopard sweat of a thousand jungle nights.

CHAPTER SIX
The Ways of Muúngu

*

As I came to know the Swahili language better
I grew more and more interested in the natives
of Africa, in these extraordinary human beings
whose lithe snake-like bodies are covered with
black skins. The very smell of them was sur-
prising, not unpleasant altogether, but bitterly
pungent, like the smoke that might rise from a
fire of faded winter weeds.

I would sit on a hillock overlooking their huts
and watch them for hours together. Old men
would come blinking out into the sunshine, old
men of an incredible age, centenarians perhaps,
with fallen jaws and wrinkled cheeks. They
would support themselves by holding to long
poles, like so many lean bears at a country fair,
the sharp blade-bones of their bowed shoulders
being covered with mottled goat-skins. Around
their gaunt legs tiny children would play, little
bare children with frog-like protruding bellies.
The women would do the work of the house-
hold. I would see them busy with a hundred
occupations: going down to the river for water,
or looking about on the edge of the plough-

land for the particular weeds they used for vegetables. Sometimes out of curiosity I would crawl through the low door of one of their huts and sit by the white ashes of the fire which is always to be found smouldering in these primitive habitations, and the inmates would offer me *posho* boiled into a sop and served in half a gourd. And observing them content there with their antique life I would be astonished, half envying them for their fortunate freedom from wry thinking. What explanation did they have for all the mysteries about them? Had some over-sagacious negro a thousand moons ago peered up at the night skies and come to the conclusion that the ultimate question could never be answered, and that it was man's wisest course to cease from speculation and enjoy, without asking questions, the delicate flavour of goat's milk, the grateful warmth of a fire, and the sweet delights of lovemaking? But there was one little matter in the ordering of their lives to which they could never be reconciled. Death! *That never failed to make them jump!* They did not at all like it when their fathers, their children, their brothers, suddenly became deaf and dumb and looked at them with imbecile

55

open mouth and awful unshut eye. To them, as to some others, the fact of Death presents itself in the light of an appalling and shocking catastrophe. In this part of Africa as soon as a man dies his corpse is abandoned and never looked upon again.

Gay, feckless, inconstant, children of sunlight and shadow, these natives are incapable of reasoning beyond the bounds of superstition. The complicated Oriental religion that has until late years satisfied Europe is far too refined and sophisticated for their woolly pates. I used to look at them going out and coming in, and I cannot tell you how remote from their methods of thought seemed to me then our intricate theology built up around that event which took place two thousand years ago on the other side of the Red Sea. *'Eloi, eloi, lama sabachthani?'* If that cry, possibly the most tragic that has ever disturbed the night-dreams of heron or owl, had reached these African valleys, I surmise that these obstinates would have given it but little attention. *'Kelele Muúngu'* ('the noise of a god') they might have muttered and then, indifferent and preoccupied, turned away to their own affairs.

The myths they possessed were extremely simple, odd traditional stories which they liked to repeat and repeat again over their camp-fires. One of these tales especially pleased me. I had been setting a trap on the other side of the escarpment and was returning along a narrow game-path not far from the place where I had had my adventure with the elephant. The native with me was a Kikuyu, tall and slim and quite naked except for the red blanket I had given him. In his right hand he held a long narrow spear, and as he walked along at the side of my pony I could not help thinking how significant, how typical, how absolutely in the right place he looked, pacing there, under the aged cedars, as his fathers had done before him for time out of mind.

Suddenly as we were advancing he pointed to a heap of dark brown matter which lay on one side of the path. 'Tembo,' he said. I looked down, and sure enough it was a heap of elephant's dung. I urged on my mule, as I felt in no mood for a second encounter with one of these animals. The Kikuyu kicked at the dry heap with his naked foot and then, turning to me, asked with the utmost gravity whether I was aware of the fact that elephants had once been men. He looked so serious when he asked the question that, on my soul, I was half inclined to believe him. I tell you in that darkening forest, with the rustling of the tropical leaves about me, and the indefinable stir of the on-coming night audible everywhere, it seemed more than possible that I was about to hear the authentic story of the origin of man.

'Long ago,' he began, 'in the days when the mountains spat fire, elephants were men. And these men were very rich. They had *ngombi, kondo, mbuzi, kuku* (cattle, sheep, goats, and chickens) in numbers like the grass on the plains. They were, indeed, so wealthy that they had no need of work. They simply lolled about all day, covering themselves with oil and red earth and making love together in the noonday heat. They had so much milk that they did not know what to do with it. Then one day one of them washed in milk, and when the others saw him they did the same thing, so that in time it became a practice with them every morning and every evening to toss this white water over their polished bodies. Well, it came to pass on a certain evening that Muúngu (God) came through

58

the forest to see if all was in order with the
animals he had created – with the rhinoceroses,
with the hyenas and with the lions, and with all
the others. And all was in order. On his way
back he suddenly caught the sound of man's
laughter and turned aside to see if they also were
well. Now it chanced that it was the time of
their evening washing, and when God saw the
good milk splash over their bodies he fell into a
great passion. "I created cows to give them the
white water of life and they now throw it away
or do worse with it." And he called the men to
him as he stood there in the shadow of the forest.
And the men, when they heard God's voice
louder than the roaring of a lion when its belly
is full, trembled and came creeping to him on
hands and knees like so many baboons. And
God cried with a loud voice : "In so much as you
have proved yourselves to be unworthy to receive
my gifts and have been guilty of this great
waste, you shall become Nyama (wild animals),
a new kind of Nyama, bearing on your heads
milk-white teeth, so that you shall be constantly
reminded of your guilt." So God transformed
them all into elephants, and they moved off
into the forest, huge grey forms with gleaming

tusks set in their bowed heads for ever and ever.'

We came to the river, crossed it, and went up the narrow mud paths leading to the boys' huts. The sun was slowly sinking towards the distant mountain slopes. The hump-backed cattle were grazing solemnly in the fenced enclosure that my brother had built for them. A boy was chopping wood outside a hut. The air was vibrant with the high-pitched sing-song of negro utterance, shrill and irresponsible.

I felt disinclined to go in just then. So, getting off my mule, I sat down on an abandoned log and began putting questions to my companion. I asked him as to our chance with regard to immortality. His answers were evasive. Obviously it was a question he did not care to discuss. I pressed him. I asked him whether he himself expected to exist after death. And then at last, under that crooked olive-tree, this child of African chaos made his sombre declaration of faith.

He told me that the sun was a one-eyed lion, who was for ever giving chase to a little white goat, the moon. That the stars were the eyes of the children of God, who, from some ultimate place of concealment, peered down upon the interminable chase. And he went on to explain that neither the one-eyed lion nor the white goat nor the sons of God troubled themselves about what goes on upon the grass-grown floor of the wild earth. Black men died and white men died and their flesh went into the bellies of hyenas, their bones remaining on the veldt for a week, a month, perhaps, to be at length either covered up by weeds or scattered abroad in the wind, so that no one might say whether or no their souls lived.

'It is *shairi Muúngu'* ('the affair of God'), he said. The lion never sleeps, the goat never sleeps. As far as the memory of man reaches, the hunt has continued; and as in the firmament above, so on the earth below, all is a perpetual pursuit, a perpetual flight. The waters of the rivers flow for ever, the leaves sprout, burgeon, and fall, old vultures die and young ones take their place, the death-hour comes at last to the strongest hippopotamus, but there are already others to replace it in the soft ooze of the lake's margin.

And as I listened to this sudden flow of sceptical speech the queerest fancies coursed through my mind. I saw the world as he saw it, saw all my industrious, ingenious, militaristic compatriots as irrelevant in the cosmic scheme, beings without scot or lot in its fleeting confusions, who had far better eat and drink and dance for their allotted span, without thought or hope or prevision for the future. 'For after all,' he concluded, 'who remembers the baboons of the escarpment who curled themselves up in the crevices to die a hundred summers ago, and yet the one-eyed lion was hunting then as he hunts to-day?'

CHAPTER SEVEN
The Death of a Dog

*

IT was about this time that rumours reached us of the fight at Longido, a hill on the German East African border. The English settlers had been beaten back and some of my brother's friends had been killed. The news made him restless, and eventually he decided to join the East African Mounted Rifles. He considered that I was quite competent to look after the farm in his absence. I confess that I was extremely reluctant to have him involved in this crazy contest, so destructive of the body-politic of civilization. I was well aware of the obstinate stupidity of the various Governments and of their culpable carelessness with regard to the magnanimous youthful spirits they held in their power. These generals, these colonels, in their spick-and-span uniforms, with the confined brainpans of a set of strutting poultry, how could one feel any confidence in such people?

On my own account I felt the future to be full of anxiety. I had come to Africa for my health, to avoid dying of consumption, and here

was I about to be transformed into a planter
pioneer, living on the outskirts of the world.
An existence that had seemed tolerable with my
brother always at hand in the case of emergency
might well, I felt, grow insupportable when
alone. He arranged for his departure on a certain Monday morning in the month of January,
1915.

On the last Sunday we went out hunting as
usual. We put up a large wart-hog in some
bushes near the house. He really was a gigantic
animal. He ran for about a mile, crossed the
river, and stood at bay in an open space. When
we came up we found him in the centre of the
pack, turning his long shining tusks first this
way and then that, and keeping all the dogs at
a safe distance. We walked towards the mêlée,
my brother with the spear he used for pig-sticking
ready in his hand. As a general rule he would
wait till the dogs had got in on the back of the
pig before using his weapon, but, even so, it
required extraordinary dexterity and strength for
the final thrust. I was never powerful enough
nor skilful enough to do it, but would content
myself with standing a little way apart, rifle in
hand. On this occasion the dogs seemed unable

to come at close quarters with the pig. He was altogether too quick for them. They made a rush at his tail, only to find that it had been replaced by his tusks. We watched for half-an-hour, but still the wart-hog stood ready for battle. My brother, tired of the long delay, came in closer. The pig caught sight of him and charged. I did not dare to shoot, for he was standing in line with the animal. I passed one agonizing moment. I saw the dogs give way and my brother steady himself, evidently intending to strike and then jump to one side. I knew how small a chance he had of succeeding in this, for a pig is as quick as lightning and can follow the slightest movement of his enemy.

I rushed forward, and then suddenly I saw a flash of white that leaped across the animal's head and made it stumble. It gave my brother his chance, and a moment later his spear had struck home and the great boar lay gasping on the ground. But there was something else lying there also. On the head of the pig, transfixed by both tusks, lay the white body of Micky. His entrails were hanging out, but he still recognized us, and as my brother stooped to free him from his agony he gave one look of wild affection. I

can see it all as clearly as though it happened yes-
terday, my brother kneeling over the small white
terrier, which lay on its side feebly wagging its
tail before its eyes closed for ever. We buried
him in an ant-bear's hole.

Monday came, and standing in the little flower
garden I watched my brother's figure on the
small grey mule disappear down the waggon
track between the plough-hands. He passed the
potato patch, the russet-coloured flax-stack, the
clump of olive-trees where we had seen our first
wild hunting dog, and then vanished from sight
completely. Immediately I was overwhelmed by
a sense of desolate loneliness. I entered the small
room to the right of the veranda which had been
his, and each object left there seemed articulate
with a kind of abject appeal, the pocket-knife he
had had since his boyhood, the old cow's horn he
used when out hunting, the bootlaces made out
of bushbuck hide and prepared by him with such
care.

Darkness fell, but my distemper increased
rather than diminished. I was enveloped by an
uneasy persistent feeling of personal loss and
came to know what nostalgia meant, that strange
physical longing for the place of one's birth, for

the familiar buildings one has grown accustomed to see about one, for the garden trees of my home, with their secure, solitary, unchanging life, for the very water-butt near the coal-house in the back yard.

Before going to bed I stepped to the rear of the house to draw some water from the rain tank. A hyena uttered its whoop on the other side of the wire fence and from far away, beyond the water-hole where the pigs drank, came uncertainly upon the night wind the moaning death-cry of some forest creature. I could hardly wait for my glass to fill; even the shadows that the clumps of geraniums threw upon the long uncut grass seemed treacherous, menacing. I slept with a loaded gun at my bed-side. From where I lay I could see dark clouds moving solemnly across the sky, and below them, below the irregular levels of the forest tree-tops, I could hear the monotonous barking of a leopard.

When at last the morning came I felt in better heart. There is always something reassuring about the first hour of the day in Africa. The jocund cries of the spur-fowl as they move on delicate clawed feet through the tropical dew, the ting-tang of the bell-bird, the incessant chat-

tering of monkeys, seem to dispel those misgivings which are so prevalent, so insistent,
during the darker hours, when one knows that,
go where one may, every game-path, every open
glen, is frequented by silent-footed shadows on
their eternal quest for blood.

CHAPTER EIGHT
A Gentleman's Rebuke

*

It became very clear to me after the departure of my brother that the gentle art of farming was by no means as easy a matter as I had at first imagined. Scarcely a day passed without my being reminded of this. For example, an evil sickness fell suddenly upon the pigs. One after another they became lame, and several had died before a settler, who happened to ride by one day, diagnosed what was wrong. They must, he said, have had access to salt, and salt, he told me, was deadly poison to pigs. This was a most startling revelation to me as to the capricious orderings of nature. I had always been led to believe that salt was necessary to the welfare of all animals. I knew that it was essential to the well-being of cattle, and I remembered clearly that a piece of rock salt, brown and round like a fragment of a human skull, had always been hung up near the left-hand bin in the stable at home. It was quite evident that I had much to learn, and I gave strict orders to the swineherd to keep his animals in the future well away from the cattle-lick. Immediately the death-rate went down and some of the pigs that were sickening recovered. This was only one of the many thousand discoveries that I made.

The dry weather set in, and even in that high forest country conditions became difficult. My rain-tank was empty and it was necessary to haul water up from the river, water which, because of the danger of dysentery, had to be boiled before it was drunk. Little thatched shelters had to be constructed at certain strategic points on the shamba so that the pigs, when they were tired of snouting for roots, could take shelter from the burning rays of the noonday sun. The veldt became dry and drab and dusty, and covered with ticks.

One morning it occurred to me that it would be a good idea to burn a certain piece of ground so that the bullocks would have the benefit of fresh grass when the heavy rains fell. I took Maniki, Abdulla, and some twenty Kikuyus, so that the fire could be kept well under control, and struck a match. In an instant flames were spreading in all directions, and I realized that the farmstead was in danger. Fire! Before that moment I had little enough conception of the inextinguishable fury of this element. Five minutes after that little wooden match had been struck great billowing clouds of smoke were being carried far up into the sky, and there before me, spreading ever wider and wider, was a tall wall of dancing flame. Fortunately the grass was thinner round the homestead and we were able to burn fire-breaks, but even so we were only just in time. Leaping and laughing in a strange passionate ecstasy the red demon I had let loose upon the tawny hide of Africa sped past unappeased. In half-an-hour the veldt at the farther end of the farm had been transformed into an unrecognizable desert of blackness, above the smouldering tussocks of which a number of hawks circled on the lookout for snakes and rats. For nearly a week afterwards, as I lay on the veranda at night, I could follow the progress of that bush-fire. I could see its thin cruel line mounting higher and higher upon the distant hills, advancing and ever advancing, eager, rapacious, unsatisfied. It fell to my lot later on to have many desperate struggles with bush-fires.

Month followed month. Sometimes for weeks together I would see only black faces. Now and again a band of trading Somalis would pass by, tall handsome men dressed in spotless linen robes. When they saw me they would leave their mules and camels and with the utmost courtesy come over to talk to me in Swahili, telling me where they were going and about the cattle they had with them. And I would ask them concerning their journey, and how long it was since they had left the walled desert cities of their land in the distant north.

On one occasion one of them came to my house benighted. He had been left behind to look for a lost donkey. He wanted to know if I would allow him to sleep on the flax stored in the great barn, and I gave him leave to do this. Late in the evening, as I sat reading *Don Quixote* (one of the seven books I had taken with me into exile), he reappeared, asking if I had an extra blanket I could lend him. And because I had already acquired the provincial attitude of a white man in a black man's country I felt disinclined to loan him any of my brother's blankets, but instead went and fetched a thick rug which was used for covering the kicking mule when the nights were chilly. You know how the occasions in one's life when one has behaved especially crudely have a way of recurring to one's mind for years and years after-wards. I offered him the wrap; he looked at it, he saw the grey hairs on it and he returned it to me in silence, but with an expression on his proud finely bred features of such infinite contempt that I felt my ignoble action had in some way put me completely outside the pale of some unwritten standard of behaviour, taken for granted amongst gentlemen in the common-wealth of the human race. Certainly my complacent Anglo-Saxon manners received a severe jolt that day, a jolt that has caused me to think twice before offering strangers who ask a favour, mule blankets!

At last the heavy rains broke and the river became a brown torrent, and the roadway a river, and each native path a stream. On the lower level of the shamba the water lay so deep and wide that from the veranda the farm would seem to be composed of a succession of ponds, and wherever one walked wide-mouthed globular African frogs croaked from out of the water. And as day after day more rain fell, Nature relaxed and awoke once more. The blackened ground that had been burnt became covered with the tenderest spring grass, upon which the zebra and kongoni collected in straggling groups. Over night, as it were, the landscape became green and the vegetable world dominant. From the ground, from the tree-tops, long green tendrils stretched and lengthened and clung and grew again. The air was redolent with the smell of sap, of a riotous fecund sap, dangerous, suffocating to all life that was not vegetable. Each early morning, as I sipped my tea, I looked out upon a land that sweated and steamed like the back of a great Shire cart-horse.

And one cold misty dawn, out of the glade which lay below the potato patch, three vast forms emerged, monstrous, primeval, and began moving slowly across to the forest — elephants! Later in the day I followed their tracks, and the way they had taken was marked by holes a foot deep, holes that were already full of water. I had no wish to come up with them, but I found it fascinating to follow in the wake of these enormous wayfarers and observe how they would advance so dexterously along the rocky side of the escarpment, nimble as cats, unconcerned apparently by the most formidable obstacles, surmounting rocks and fallen trees with little or no difficulty. Ha! Ha! I thought, here are the true ancient lords and masters of the vegetable world. Through the densest jungles of the forest they made their roads, and on each side saplings would be broken and the branches of the trees thrown to the ground. Every day during that time Nature would seem to me more and more insurgent, till I got the feeling that the small fragment of cultivated ground which it was my business to tend was like a tiny unstable island threatened on all sides by invincible tidal waves. Yet there were certain moments when, in spite of all my agitations, I was able to appreciate the full significance of that extraordinary scene, when I became amazingly aware of the vast indrawing and outdrawing of the breath of Nature, of Nature sluggish, potential, unbridled, as ever she had been before her witty and wilful offspring had learned to harness her for his own ends.

CHAPTER NINE
The Leopard Trap

*

ONE afternoon as I was walking back from the shamba Abdulla met me full of talk about having seen a herd of waterbuck at the top of the escarpment. As all the boys wanted meat, I determined to take my gun and try to shoot one of the animals. I have always been a poor sportsman. During the holidays at home, while my brother would go about, shot-gun under his arm, on the lookout for rabbits or wood-pigeons, I would wander off for long rambling walks with nothing more dangerous than an ash-plant in my hand.

I now sent a boy for my rifle, and with Abdulla as guide crossed the swollen river. The forest was saturated with moisture. The maidenhair ferns that grew out of the black pristine leaf-mould were drenched; the trunks of the trees had grown black with dampness, and at every step heavy drops of water fell from the grey beards of lichen above our heads. It took us longer than usual to reach the top of the escarpment. The game-paths were slippery and overgrown.

As soon as we emerged from the forest and

began crossing the high open levels of the escarpment we advanced more carefully, making our way from one clump of bushes to another. The long brown grass of the dry season had vanished and its place had been taken by the rich green herbage of an English park. Abdulla went forward swiftly, stealthily. He was approaching the place where he had seen the animals grazing from the valley below, *kuru* (waterbuck) – in his opinion the best eating of all the African buck.

I followed behind. I believe I was more occupied in watching my companion than in looking out for the game. There was something extremely revealing in Abdulla's stooping, rapidly moving gait. All his senses were alert. He had been transformed from a simple good-natured negro to a hunting animal. There was a sharp diabolic expression in his black eyes and a deadly secretive concentration about his attitudes. He represented man in search for blood under the most primitive conditions, man before he had evolved that complicated cold-hearted system by which animals are bred up from their birth with calculating ingenuity for the knife.

Suddenly he stopped and stood stock-still, as Ugonjwa was in the habit of doing when he had

77

marked down a covey of quail. I peered round the bush behind which we were hidden and there, not more than fifty yards away, stood some half-dozen waterbuck. They had no suspicion of danger. I put my rifle to my shoulder and pulled the trigger. They were away in an instant, their rough shaggy shanks moving up and down with the jerky movement that is characteristic of these animals. They had gone only a short distance, however, when one of their number, the young bull at which I had aimed, fell and lay struggling in the grass. With a savage incoherent cry Abdulla leapt forward. He was on its back in an instant, and with one horn held firmly in his large-fingered hand, he slowly and deliberately forced his knife through the tough hide of the animal's neck and cut its throat.

He now left to fetch some Kikuyus to help him carry back the meat. I meanwhile crossed the escarpment to my favourite ledge overlooking the El Bordossat valley. The high mountain slopes opposite, twenty miles away, looked more romantic than ever, now that they were green. Certainly one would never have believed that there was treachery abroad on these 'delectable mountains.' And yet well I knew that by the time I was eating my supper secure in my stone house a thousand sharp eyes would be peering through the rank verdure that grew on each side of those far-off lawns. Blood! Blood! Blood! how tireless, how merciless, was the unending pursuit of that divine elixir! Night after night it continued while an indifferent wind went whimpering through the thorn bushes and a haggard moon floated on and on behind black and broken clouds.

It was already twilight by the time I had re-crossed the river and passed the patch of Indian corn which Maniki had planted at the foot of the cattle yards. The boys were making merry over the meat. I could hear their cries of exultation as the red flesh was distributed. There seemed to be an unusual stir in my own house. The next moment I saw a white man's figure issue from behind the kitchen shanty. It was my brother Willie! He had been allowed a week's leave. In a moment all my anxieties, all my worries vanished.

The last three days of his holiday were occu-pied by him in building a box-trap. For some reason he had a mania for catching a leopard alive and he spent much time in the forest split-

79

ting cedar logs. When he considered that he had split enough he had them conveyed to the water-hole where the pigs drank, and began building the trap. He sank each post some two feet into the ground and in this way constructed a kind of small shed, which he roofed with other logs nailed to the uprights. Behind this shed he built a smaller one, where the bait was to be placed. The ground near the logs separating the two enclosures had a false bottom, which at the slightest pressure would release a trigger peg attached in some way to a long pole that held the heavy gate in position, a gate that would come rattling down as soon as it was released. I used to laugh at my brother for wasting his time over this contrivance. It seemed to me incredible that any leopard would ever venture into such a place. Unluckily my brother had to go away before the thing was finished. He explained it all to me, however, and extracted a formal promise that I would give it a trial. It was completed three days after he left. I borrowed a young goat and, as I had been instructed, put it into the inner enclosure.

The very next morning, if you please, as I was taking some store pigs out of the yards

THE LEOPARD TRAP

I heard the excited voice of a boy running up from the shamba shouting, *'Chui! Chui! Chui!'* I was by no means pleased. It was no joke for a consumptive, whose natural inclinations lay in the direction of books, to be suddenly called upon to kill a leopard in a box-trap. I thought I had best supplement my ignorance with regard to fire-arms by having a good supply of them at hand. I took with me a rifle, a shotgun, and a Winchester repeater. I approached the cedar logs with the utmost suspicion. The posts were placed only two inches apart, so it was impossible to see between them unless one was close up. Indeed, I had come up to within a yard of the trap before I detected the large angry yellow head of the beast. It was looking straight at me, and I shall not easily forget the strange thrill that went down my spine as I met the cold concentrated gaze of that imprisoned cat. I shot. A second afterwards I realized that my worst fears were likely to be fulfilled. The cage shook and rocked and a succession of deafening roars issued from behind the logs. Sometimes I thought the sides of the trap were going to give way, sometimes the roof. I moved from one position to another, trying in vain to get a steady shot. It was useless; the animal went round and round like a demented squirrel. Suddenly I heard the noise of breaking wood and saw a large paw protrude and begin tearing and wrenching at an unsound log. Splinters began to fly, and I realized that it would require only a few minutes before it would be out. The natives fled. I seized my shot-gun. It was loaded with S.S.G. I fired, and then, misery upon misery, I realized that I had only succeeded in blowing away still more of the broken log. The explosion, however, had one good result: it set the leopard once more upon its gyrations, giving me an opportunity, and a very welcome opportunity, to get to the other side, the side exactly opposite from the dangerous aperture. Once more the scraping and tearing commenced, but before the log gave I crept close up and, putting the barrel of my weapon actually against the fur of the animal's shoulder, pulled the trigger and shot it dead.

It was a very large leopard, with a fine pelt, which, incidentally, was completely ruined by me in my first effort of curing a skin. I never reset the damned trap. Two years afterwards, as I was riding by the farm, I made a digression for the purpose of looking at the place of this naïve adventure. The trap was still standing, but it resembled a child's garden-arbour, so overgrown was it with tangled creepers.

CHAPTER TEN
The Great Rift Valley

*

To the right of the forest farm, across a valley opposite the escarpment, about ten miles away, rose a high range of hills, rough, rocky, and broken with trees. Often towards evening I would stroll across to a flat stone promontory a few hundred yards from my small house to look at that black outline of hills. For some reason it fascinated me, perhaps because the natives would often point in its direction and say *'baya sana,'* or 'very bad,' indicating that its recesses were infested with wild and dangerous animals. On such occasions they would imitate the abrupt snorting noise of a charging rhinoceros.

In the broad daylight I would look at that distant range quite casually. It seemed then, as I trudged behind the straining bullocks, hoof-deep in the fecund brown earth of the shamba, as if it made an appropriate background to the farm, to those few acres of isolated cultivation. But at night-fall it was different. It became a kind of habit with me to sit for half-an-hour each evening on that projecting promontory

84

paved with flat rocks. No grass grew on it and its cracked bare levels were the favourite haunt of jackals, who would slink up after dark to howl there at the moon with uplifted pointed chins. I would go to the place after I had given out the boys' rations late in the afternoon, and as the temperature fell with the oncoming night the atmosphere would grow tainted with the sour-sweet smell of burning logs, and whenever I chanced to turn my head from that tremendous horizon I would see between contorted tree-trunks more and more clearly the intermittent, reassuring flicker of the hut fires.

As the weeks passed, those distant hills began to obsess my imagination. I became afraid of them, afraid of their undisturbed loneliness, and yet at the same time I felt more and more insistent upon me a desire to explore their obscure retreats, to stand on this or that high craggy peak, at the foot of which, on certain clear mornings, I would fancy I actually saw mysterious black forms moving.

At last I took a day off, and with Abdulla at my side rode across the intervening valley. We experienced some difficulty in scaling the mountain slopes, the path we took being treacherous

85

and often leading to inaccessible clefts up which my mule could not possibly clamber. In all directions we saw the tracks of pachyderms, tracks that had been made months before, and tracks so fresh that the stalks of certain succulent plants still oozed sap from the places where they had been crushed or broken. From dim leafy nurseries far up above our heads came the chattering of monkeys, and the clang, clang of harsh-throated birds whose exultant screaming fractured the cool tropical atmosphere till the gaudy orange trumpet flowers seemed themselves to be emitting a shrill music. Presently we passed through a ravine so sheltered by woven vine-leafed creepers that for centuries no splashes of sunlight had warmed the dark mould into which my mule's narrow hoofs sunk.

Once above the forest belt, however, we were able to advance more rapidly. My purpose was, if possible, to climb to the top of a high crag, the broken yellow side of which was a conspicuous landmark from the jackal promontory. I found that this particular crag was much farther away than I had anticipated. The downlands we had to cross to reach it were covered with a red grass which at a little distance took the appearance of English oats, rusty-coloured, and ready for the reapers. Across these wide mountain spaces large herds of zebra were grazing, with here and there a heavy-headed kongoni buck loping in their wake, while ever and again, far up above them in the clear dazzling sky, came the yelping of an African eagle.

At the foot of the crag I off-saddled the mule and ate the cold wing of a spur-fowl, some honey sandwiches, and some Kikuyu bananas. The honey had been given to me by a Wondorobo three days before. He had brought it to me in a gourd, a curious black substance full of the legs and abdomens of wild bees, proving by their presence that even after the sagacious honey-bird had directed the man to the right tree he had had considerable difficulty in wresting from the infuriated insects their sweet treasure.

There was a small spring near where we sat, and after I had finished eating I went to it to drink and bathe my hair and beard in its coolness. Abdulla soon followed my example, splashing the water over his black muscular thighs. Meanwhile, the grey mule browsed on the rushes at the pool's edge, moving its tail to and fro, and now and again lifting up its head to give us one of those slow, shrewd, calculating glances that are so characteristic of these sly hybrids. In the centre of the pool was a flat rock, which rose just a few inches above the water. The surface of this rock was completely covered by a fluttering, quivering veil of butter-flies, butterflies of every colour – yellow, red, and Prussian blue – which opened and shut their damask wings in the sharp heat. Whether they also had been moistening their delicate parched tongues in that grey ferny place and had now set-tled on the rock in an ecstasy of gratitude, of dainty well-being, I could not tell; but the spec-tacle of this flimsy, frivolous, super-refined gather-ing, so impossibly fragile, so impossibly lovely, in a most strange way startled me into appreciating the outlandish sophistication of a continent capable of producing, after its own amazing fashion, such abnormal contrasts as are presented to the eye by the appearance of a gorbellied rhinoceros and the decorative beauty of the shim-mering denizens of that parched stone.

After a while I left Abdulla and the mule and began to climb the crag. The grass was slippery. When I reached that part of the ascent where the rocky crest rose abruptly from the slopes I moved round the crag's base, looking for some chimney which might help me to clamber to the very top. I found what I wanted, and slowly, step by step, made the ascent. The astonished rock-rabbits scuttled out of my way or peered at me inquisitively from the mouth of some obscure fissure. As I looked at their excited eyes, black as ivy berries, I could almost hear them interrogating each other as to the purpose which could possibly have brought this pale deliberate gorilla to invade their lofty isolated retreats.

At last I pulled myself over the topmost boulder and found that I was standing on a perfectly flat lawn some fifty yards long. And what a panorama now lay before me! For the first time I was looking down upon the great Rift Valley, upon that extraordinary crack in the earth's surface which is said to stretch from the Victoria Nyanza, across the Red Sea, into the heart of Mesopotamia. And fair, indeed, the fertile valley looked on that bright noonday, backed on one side by the frowning slopes of Eburu and on the other by the bold contours of the Mau Mountains. I could see Lake Nakuru to the right, and at the foot of where I stood, so that it seemed I could almost toss a pebble into its amethystine waters, lay Lake Elmenteita, while far off on the left I could dimly discern the papyrus-grown shores of Lake Naivasha. And between each gleaming inland sea, lying like the forgotten shields of heroes on the emerald veldt, sprang sharp, jagged volcanoes, volcanoes whose outlines resembled, as they rose out of those wide expanses of pastureland, the pointed broken fangs of gigantic buried wolves.

Indeed, so wide, so radiant, so transformed did the great Rift Valley appear to me that when I turned my head to mark the dark upland forest farm where I lived, with the corrugated-iron roof actually visible, a tiny shining speck amid that ocean of green, I felt an unexpected longing for the newer prospect. I wanted to be riding over those broad plains which were lying there so placidly in the sunshine. I wanted to be riding along the silver-white shores of those becalmed lakes, to be living in a land which once a day received the angular, cubistic shadows of those extinct craters.

NOT long after this excursion I heard rumours that a manager was required for a farm right on the very shore of Lake Elmenteita, and by the end of August I found myself established in a hut overlooking those strange waters. I had loaded a Dutch cart with all my own and my brother's belongings, and simply migrated, following behind the yoked oxen as they dragged the heavy creaking waggon along the old caravan road down which I had so often seen the Somali traders disappear.

My duties from now till I left Africa four years later were far more exacting than they had been. The farm for which I was responsible was one of the largest and wildest in the country. It was a stock farm of thirty thousand acres, which afforded grazing for two thousand head of cattle and fourteen thousand sheep. The hut in which I lived was built of wattle and daub, and resembled an Irish cabin. It had two doors, a mud floor, and three apertures which served as windows. I used to breakfast under the shadow of a rough grass roof, and from where I sat I could look out upon the lake.

As I had anticipated, the Rift Valley was completely different from the country which surrounded the forest farm. The very grass that covered its rich alluvial soil was different, a kind of low-creeping knotted couch-grass quite unlike the red variety which grew in the highlands. And the wild life of the valley was more plentiful than I had ever known, more plentiful than I had ever conceived to be possible. As I sipped my tea innumerable gazelles would be grazing within rifle-shot, enormous dragon-faced ostriches tiptoeing their way between the low lilishwa bushes. Sometimes I would watch a wart-hog sow leading her young ones along the road which wound from my hut to the cattle yards, and sometimes the baboons would come and hold parliament about the troughs outside the sheds, balancing themselves on the edge of the water-tank, or climbing on to the rails, or crawling on all fours to peer at me through the scrub, knowingly, sapiently. And towards evening great lubberly Egyptian geese would come from the lake to see if they could not pick up some morsels of meal that might have dropped out of the boxes which were carried each night to the sheds where the bulls were kept.

There were a number of ponies on the ranch, but the two I used to ride most often were Ramadan, an Arab stallion, and Rosinante, a small white country-bred gelding. Several days went by before I had time to go down to the lake, and then one Sunday afternoon, after I had put my labour books in order, I set out with Shafara, the head Masai. A low line of kopjes lay between the homestead and its shore, and between each kopje was a grassy rock-strewn glade which sloped down to the smooth lawns that separated the mimosa-trees at the water's edge from the hill-side. I had not walked far down one of these glades before I noticed that the ground was littered with little heaps of grass, damp and sticking together, and looking as if they might have fallen from the choked knives of some enormous mowing machine. I was puzzled, and pointed them out to my companion. *Kiboko!* Hippopotamus! It was perfectly true. Each of these mounds of crushed fodder marked the place where one of these gigantic midnight feeders had let food drool out from his square, flat, bristled lips. I was thrilled. From my

93

earliest childhood these great river-horses had seemed to me of all animals the most romantic, dividing their time, as they do, between the dimly lit watery levels of the lake's bottom and the cool dark pastures of a moon-irradiated world. When once we were through the mimosa-trees and had come out upon the sandy shore we found traces enough of them. The smooth white surface against which the poisoned waters lapped retained countless indentures of their round flat feet. But look about me as I might I could see none of them. Where had they gone, I wondered, these stupendous amphibians. Was it really possible that they were at that very moment meandering about with lowered heads on the broad acreages that must lie below that still flat stretch of sparkling water, or were they, perhaps, spending the somnolent drowsy Sunday hours couchant amongst the rushes which grew upon the opposite shore four miles away? That first visit to Lake Elmenteita made a deep impression upon my mind. What other country but Africa could have nurtured these mimosa-trees, with their elongated branches from which fell, as from the stationary bodies of serpents, luxuriant festoons in a thousand incongruous growths? And

94

characteristically enough there was not a trunk, a bough, a twig even, of these trees but projected thorns, long, and stiff, and sharp as darning-needles.

Certainly, standing there on that lonely shore with the naked herdsman at my side, listening to the haunted cries of the water-birds, long-legged, long-beaked, that circled about us, listening to the evil lapping of the water against the crisp margin, like the tongue of a satiate lion, I felt, however much hereafter I might be submerged by the vulgar modern world, the world of motor-cars, and factories, and telephones, and 'movies', I would never be able to forget the fact that I had once, upon a certain afternoon, stood looking out upon a portion of the earth's surface that still retained evidence of God's tremendous creative genius. I felt like the first mortal who, wandering far from the Asiatic nursery of his race, had been privileged, with uplifted head, to scrutinize the dark secrets of this great continent, which for so long had remained undisturbed by aught but the presence of fabulous saurians lolling and gambolling together in solitary Equatorial sunshine.

On our way back we noticed that a plot of

land lately planted with Indian corn on this side
of a deep ravine had been invaded by baboons.
It looked as if a whole township of dwarfs had
entered the enclosure. As soon as we approached,
the sentinel baboons gave the alarm, uttering
bass guttural sounds. Immediately the whole
mob ambled across a narrow ford and went up
through the scrub towards the forest. I ran as
fast as I could towards the side of the ravine and
took a random shot at a big animal that was
bringing up the rear. It fell. There was no possible means of crossing the ravine just there, so I
told Shafara to go round. The monkey had fallen
behind a bush and was completely hidden from
us, and I suspected that Shafara considered he
was being sent upon a fool's errand. After waiting for a quarter of an hour I observed him
approaching the place I had indicated on the
other side of the ravine, and a moment later saw
him stoop and pick up something from the
ground. It was a baby baboon which he had
found clinging to the hairy back of its dead
mother. Though the tiny creature had been
puzzled that she had sunk down so suddenly, it
had still continued to cling to her, expecting, no
doubt, that she would get up in a few minutes

and carry it back to the forest after the others, as she had so often done before.

The small animal was very quaint to look at. It was covered all over with black fluff and possessed perfectly shaped infinitesimal hands. At first, when it felt itself being held by strangers, by baboons that were no baboons, it kept giving odd spasmodic jumps. I carried it back to the house. That evening it would take no food, but remained quite silent. I began to fear it was going to die, as happens so often with wild forest animals when they are taken captive. I put a belt round its waist and tied it with a piece of string to the leg of my camp bed. The next morning I was wakened by the most bewitching chatter. I gave it milk and it drank until its small body grew as round as a bottle. From that moment I won its affection. We were seldom separated afterwards. It would ride with me all day long on the front of my saddle, and when I was in the house stay clinging to me, under my coat, holding with its hands to my waistcoat pocket. At meals its head would peep out of its hiding-place and I would feed it on lumps of sugar or anything that it seemed to fancy. It would then croon at me. In time I came to know its language, its sound of love, anger, fear, and mischief. I was enchanted by its personality and fell completely under its influence. It was extremely clever. It could drink from a cup without upsetting the milk, could unwind its chain if entangled, could open biscuit tins, and could pull my dog's tail without getting bitten. Once I went on *safari* for a month. When I returned I expected that Tony, my monkey, would have forgotten me. Not a bit of it! The moment he caught sight of my white pony he rushed down his pole screaming with excitement. For nearly two hours he kept up a flow of welcoming talk, burying his head against me. When I left Africa he was already a half-grown monkey. He died in 1922. I would not care to confess how troubled I was by the thought that I was separated for ever and ever from this little orphan of Africa whose mother I had murdered.

CHAPTER TWELVE
The Death of a Lion

*

WEEKS and months passed rapidly enough on the Rift Valley Farm. Every hour of the day was occupied. It was necessary to keep the most accurate counts of the various flocks so as to prevent sheep-stealing. I was continually finding myself leaning over a gate or hurdle while hundreds upon hundreds of these singularly stupid animals shouldered their way through the narrow exit I held open. Three, six, nine, twelve, fifteen, I would murmur as that never-ending stream of woolly backs spilled itself out upon the open veldt. Whenever I came to the odd number of the hundred I would exchange a tally stick from one hand to the other. And all the time the smell of the sheep would rise up from the enclosure, from the soft dust of the boma which had been churned into a fine powder by the pressure of so many pointed, cloven feet, breaking up the hard morsels of sheep's dung; and flies would collect on the hot timber rails, and as I counted and counted, dazed, yet apprehensive lest I should make a slip, a thousand unreal dreams would flit across my mind. As soon as the counting was done I would go over to the huts where the boys slept, huts some three feet high, made of lilishwa branches, with interiors as compact and snug as so many tom-tits' nests, and I would talk to the herder and see how many skins of dead sheep he had pegged out to dry, not forgetting to deduct these when I made my final calculations sitting under the shade of a neighbouring caper-tree.

My anxiety over the cattle was also considerable. They would be perpetually getting gall-sickness, and I would have to dose them with Epsom salts, shoving the bottle into the beast's mouth while a number of boys held it still and I embraced its long-shaped head with my left arm. The natives, in order to get meat, would play a thousand evil tricks upon the cattle. They would tell me a steer had died of some mysterious sickness, and when I rode up to the place where it lay I would find that they had killed it by pouring boiling water down its throat or puncturing its intestines by thrusting a sharp stick up its anus. In my wrath I would then doctor the carcass with prussic acid so that none of the boys would dare to eat any of the meat, and it would remain untouched by man; but the vultures would come down in black clouds, huge griffin vultures, and also the smaller species so happily named 'Pharaoh's chickens,' and these hideous moulting dusty-looking fowls would gorge themselves and flutter and die, while others less unfortunate would sit gulping and replete on the soiled branches of near-by trees.

Soon after the breaking of the light rains at the end of October my brother arrived on a fortnight's leave. He was eager to shoot a lion, but go where he might he could find no trace of these animals. Eventually, at the end of the first week, he decided to ride over to visit a friend of his near Naivasha. He did not expect to get back for three days. The day he left the sky was overcast, and by two in the afternoon it began to rain. It rained and rained, and towards nightfall, when I walked down to the store to give out the boys' rations, the general look of things was extremely depressing. A raw cold wind blew gustily from the direction of the forest, carrying with it a continual downpour. A cold soughing desolation seemed to have settled over the land, and the lake itself looked uninspired, windswept, dun-coloured. Darkness fell, but still the rain and wind continued. I went to bed early.

I could have slept only a few hours when I was wakened by a strange noise. It sounded as if a charge of cavalry was thundering past my house. I leapt out of bed and hastily bolted the two doors that stood opposite each other. At first I could not tell what the devil to make of it, and then, quite close, not more than thirty yards away, I heard the snort of a terrified ox. I guessed at once what had happened. The two hundred head of bullocks, which were camped three miles away under the forest, had stampeded and were careering back to the homestead. I knew that lions must be abroad. Indeed, it was just such a night that these animals naturally choose for their depredations. I was perfectly right in my conjecture. Dawn had scarcely broken before a native herder was standing at my door to say that *simba nkwisha pigga moja gombi* ('a lion has killed a bullock'). I rode with him to the place. The mangled animal lay at the bottom of a dry river-bed. Its neck had been broken and the skin on the side of its head showed plainly the marks of the lion's claws. Obviously the lion had leapt on the terrified creature's back and in the desperate rush that ensued had dislocated the steer's neck with its outstretched paw.

At any time that dry river-bed would have been an ugly place enough, but now with the torn body lying there I did not at all care for the look of it. The bullock's head retained in death the same agonized look that it had borne when it had sunk struggling to the ground a few hours before. Its tongue, that broad tongue which had drawn in so many mouthfuls of harmless couch-grass, was now hanging out, and from under the horns the glazed eyes stared blankly, abjectly, at the steep bank of the ravine. The lion had stripped one flank of its hide, and the ribs, crushed and broken off, were protruding.

What was I to do? I knew well that when once a lion has taken to killing cattle it will do an incredible amount of harm. I remembered an old rusty iron trap I had seen leaning against the wall of the store. When I got back I gave instructions to have it conveyed to the place. It was an enormous gin and required two boys to lift it from the ground. That day I rode to a distant sheep camp and did not get back till late in the afternoon. Very carefully I began setting the trap, covering its teeth with scraps of dry cow-dung and leaves. It took me much longer than I had expected. Darkness began to gather in the dry river-bed. I wished myself anywhere but just where I was. As I fumbled with the rusty bolts I grew more and more nervous. It is a habit of a lion never to go far from a fresh kill, and I was well acquainted with this fact. They drink their victim's blood, eat a few of the choicest pieces of meat, and lie up in the immediate vicinity till the following evening. Presently the curious, sour, foxy smell that pervaded the *donga,* the penetrating unmistakable smell of lion, fairly got on my nerves. Now that all was so nearly ready I was reluctant to leave the place before actually setting the trap, and yet the more jumpy I grew the more difficult I found it to manipulate the iron screws.

Suddenly I heard something moving through some bushes at the top of the bank. I was on my feet in an instant, and then to my utter amazement came the voice of my brother calling my name. Never had I felt more relieved. The tension was over, all my fear gone. We laughed and jested. The wretched river-bed lost its sinister power. What mattered it whether the lion was stretching itself, was beginning to move about uneasily, now that my brother was at my side?

The next morning news came in that the trap had disappeared, completely vanished. We soon found the open place leading from the river-bed up which the lion had made its escape. We tracked it for about a mile across the veldt to where it had entered the forest. Here the dangerous part of the pursuit began, for we had no dogs with us and the density of the foliage offered many places of ambush for the lion. I suggested leaving it to itself, trap and all, but my brother would not hear of such a thing. Foot by foot we crawled through the brushwood. It was impossible to stand up. I could see where certain obtruding roots had been scraped by the trap and every second I anticipated a sudden attack. On we went, my brother first, myself second, and two Kikuyus bringing up the rear. It was the devil's own occupation, this crawling on hands and knees into the jaws of an infuriated lion. At last we came to a narrow glade grown high with elephant-grass. Our advance here was equally dangerous, but the mere fact of standing upright made one feel better. We came to a spot where the lion had been rolling angrily, trying to rid its

paw of the trap. The yellow grass was beaten
down. Still we advanced. Soon we once more
entered the forest. We now walked from tree to
tree slowly, cautiously. And then it came, the
tremendous challenging roar of our enemy! In
a single second the two Kikuyus were up trees,
and on my soul I could hardly blame them. The
mere volume of the sound was appalling. It
seemed to shake the very cedar-trees to their
deepest roots. It must have been audible a dozen
miles away. The fact that I had voluntarily
manœuvred myself into close quarters with an
animal capable of emitting such a hullabaloo
seemed to me then the most utter folly. At
length the reverberation subsided. I still had seen
nothing of the lion, and in the ensuing silence
the forest resumed its appearance of emptiness.
Slowly my brother went forward, his gun held
in readiness. Suddenly I saw him raise it to his
shoulder and shoot. The report of his rifle was
followed immediately by an ugly growl, and an
enormous snarling yellow body raised itself above
the undergrowth and with heavy impeded movements came plunging towards us. Twenty yards,
ten yards, and then my brother shot again, and to
my deep satisfaction the white-fanged, black-

maned monster rolled over dead not five yards away.

It was a magnificent animal in all the glory and splendour of its prime. And what strength! In its last terrible fury it had made no more of that trap than if it had been a boxing-glove, and now, for all its valour, it lay there stretched out on the maidenhair fern, done to death by the merciless weapon of a subtle and ingenious enemy. Sitting on its shoulder, examining its eyelids, its teeth, its rough prickly tongue, I could not but think of the wild manner of that life cut short so abruptly. Those ears; how often had they not heard the last shrill shriek of a zebra, of a waterbuck, resonant as a taut tambourine under the awful stroke of its paw. Those small-pupiled eyes; what violent destruction of life had they not looked upon in forest or plain, under the still, indifferent star-shine of Canopus.

CHAPTER THIRTEEN
An African Artist
*

DURING those years in the Rift Valley I came to know in a most intimate way the moods and manners of the various natives who were working for me. The Masai struck me as being by far the most interesting of the tribes with which I had to do. I employed a number of this arrogant and ancient race in the capacity of herders. I was never tired of admiring their actual physical shapeliness. With their supple limbs and haughty aristocratic features they suggested in each graceful movement of their bodies a troop of godlike Spartans who long years ago had strayed into Africa to become bronzed by the tropical sun.

Deep in his heart every Masai feels nothing but contempt for Europeans. Unlike the Kavirondo and Kikuyu they can never be persuaded to wear any article of the white man's dress. They hold that we have conquered them not by superior courage but by the invention of tricky weapons. Yes, they are a strange people, these Masai. To this very day they live on flesh and blood, regarding a vegetable diet as despicable and fit only for Kikuyus and monkeys. When they are thirsty the Masai shoot arrows into the necks of their oxen and catch the trickling blood in a gourd; and when they are hungry they drive a steer to some concealed river-bed and kill and eat it there. I was never tired of listening to the stories they recounted of their old triumphant days before the appearance of that redoubtable shopkeeper, Mr. Mackinnon, and the 'floating' of the East African Trading Company. I would listen to these tales over their camp-fires with the black dome of night above my head and the little intimate dancing flames before my eyes: I would listen to them lying on a shaded rock in the hot noon-day, a rock whose smooth surface still bore upon it certain symmetrical markings scratched out, perhaps centuries before, by some indolent pro-genitor of the herdsman for the quaint game of forest checkers played with smooth stones. On these occasions my imagination would be stirred into a kind of clairvoyance and I would see these proud invincible savages, these *Il-Muran,* these warriors, swiftly passing in long lines over the tanned lion-skin of the veldt till they came at the hour before dawn to the doomed village of their enemy. I would hear the wild cries of the victors, the screams of the dying, see the wavering veils of smoke above the licking, elated flames; and then, returning with them to their *Manyattas,* behind the fat herds of stolen cattle, be present when their treble-voiced maidens came out to meet them, gleeful, wild with love. In those days the raiding area of the Masai stretched from Somaliland to the coast town of Mombasa. For generations they remained the undisputed lords of the country, a handful of merciless lions abroad amongst fat-tailed sheep!

Very different are the Kikuyu. For years they have tried to ape the demeanour and customs of the Masai, but without success. They are gay, good-natured, feckless, but lack the cold, truculent audacity of their old-time foes. The Masai steal cattle and sheep, but nothing else. The Kikuyu steal cattle and sheep and anything else they can lay their hands upon. You can trust a Masai to stand by you in a tight corner. The Kikuyu will be off, out of sight, up a tree, at the first whistle of danger. You can strike a Kikuyu with impunity, but if you strike a Masai you had best knock him senseless, or you will most surely receive six inches of cold steel in your belly.

The curled contemptuous lips of the Masai are filled with crisp proverbs and fine picturesque oaths such as it would be hard to imagine issuing from the jocund broad mouth of a 'Kuke.' 'May you never spit white again' was an exclamation the full significance of which I, as a consumptive, particularly appreciated. 'May you trip up and turn blue' was a sinister and realistic reference to the curious colour that the face of a negro assumes after death has taken place. 'A zebra cannot lose his stripes' always struck me as being a good African version of an ancient piece of wisdom. And what courage the Masai have, what terrible, deadly courage! Shafara, my own head boy, met his death in the following horrible fashion. He worked for me for two years and then went away on leave. On reaching the reserve he discovered that a man-eating lion had been giving trouble. Each day the *Il-Muran* went out to look for it and each day it evaded them. Then one afternoon as Shafara was coming back alone from the hunt he was met by a crowd of screaming women, who declared that the great beast had actually entered the village and disappeared through the doorway of Shafara's own hut, where his aged mother, a blind woman, was bedridden.

Shafara was carrying a short native spear, and without a moment's thought he crawled into the darkened place. Consider the bravery required for an action like that! Think of the audacity of creeping after a lion like a stoat after a rabbit. The battle must have been appalling! Naked man against naked beast. These native huts with their pointed grass roofs are as dark as cellars, and round and round the dingy cave the two rolled. The noise, they told me, was deafening. With tooth and claw the beast bit and tore at the man, while he with his short sword stabbed and stabbed at the yellow, infuriated body. When at last it was over they found the animal dead and Shafara lying at his last gasp near the old woman he had defended. The event troubled me a good deal at the time. I was fond of Shafara and depended much on his advice in everything that concerned the cattle. Curiously enough, the last time we had been together we had spoken of death. We were walking past a certain caper-tree, and for some reason it came into my head to tell him of a certain whimsical fancy of mine –

nothing less, in fact, than that, in the case of my dying in the country, he would see to it that I was buried at just this spot, in sight of the lake, and not far from the baboon-haunted ravine. He had listened to my talk and then, after giving me a curious scrutinizing look, had spoken these words: *'Sisi sasa kanga, sisi hapana jua siku ndege eupi taka kula'* ('We are as the guinea-fowl and do not know in what hour the white-breasted hawk will devour us'). I cannot tell how it was, but something in the intonation of his voice seemed to me oracular. Did we both, I afterwards wondered, standing there in the bright sunshine, hear the echo of his impending doom? Is it really possible, as some men say, that the fate of an individual casts a palpable shadow as it approaches?

The Kikuyu are as a general rule more super-stitious than the Masai and, it may be, more sen-sitive also. I once came upon a real artist among them. He was a young boy with a deformed leg, but with something pleasing about his face. Pos-sibly it was on account of this appealing look that I 'wrote him on' as a general labourer. He gave me a great deal of trouble. From the first he was listless. For example, if a sheep got into difficulties when we were dipping I would be quite sure that Masharia would be the last of the boys to notice that anything was wrong. Probably he would be standing on the edge of the bath, plunger in hand, oblivious of his surroundings, thinking of, God only knew what. I used to become furious and would often enough strike at him with my whip. It was just the same when the boys were out in the shamba cutting mealies. If I rode round to see how the work was progressing I would be sure to find that Masharia was doing nothing, watching the baboons, perhaps, as they moved about on the veldt opposite scraping for roots. Or if it was not the baboons he would be gazing absently at the crystalline water of Lake Elmenteita as it took to itself more and more colour in the slanting sunlight. On seeing me he would bend to his work with exaggerated energy, and I would perhaps pass by without saying anything, or may be wake him up by riding after him till all the other boys laughed to see their crippled comrade jump so nimbly over the green bundles already wilting in the dry heat. After a time I began to think I would really have to get rid of him. He did not seem worth his wages of five rupees a month.

Then one fine morning, brutalized though I had become by these devilish tropics, I recognized him for what he was.

I was in the yards drafting a herd of bullocks. I was taking off the larger beasts to send down to the Indian slaughter-houses in Nairobi. It was exhausting work. The cattle kept bunching up against the sides of the stockade while with blows and cries we tried to separate them. Each time they moved they sent into the air a cloud of dust which choked and blinded us. There were about half-a-dozen boys in the yards working with me, but, even so, we were short of hands. Suddenly I realized that Masharia was not present. I asked where he was, but nobody seemed to know. Leaving the boys to get on as best they could I went to look for him in the huts. He lived in a small wooden building built originally for a store. As I had been short of native accommodation I had allowed Masharia to use it. On approaching I noticed that smoke was issuing from the eaves and concluded at once that he was engaged in cooking food instead of coming out to work. I made up my mind that this would be the last time he would fool me. I would have it out with him once for all, I thought.

I came up to the door and looked in. He was not eating, he was simply tracing rude pictures with a piece of charcoal upon the wall of his house. He had not heard me, and for a few moments I stood watching him. He was working with absorbed interest, his black fingers trembling in his excitement. Do you know, when I at last entered that tiny habitation I found that its four walls were simply covered with drawings! For the most part they represented pictures of the world by which he was surrounded, pictures of that queer visible world which is made up of human beings dark as Satan, of lions, of hippos, of serpents, of bearded goats, and of everything else that moves over the surface of Africa. The draughtsmanship was, of course, crude, but the work was executed with such spirit that I stood speechless. There was I myself done to life, a bearded monster on the top of a hideous quadruped, out of whose nostrils fire issued. 'Ha! ha!' it seemed to be neighing, after the manner of the war-horses of Israel.

I left him and went back to the yards. But as the heavy bullocks plunged and snorted in the dust-filled enclosure my mind kept reverting over and over again to this strange child of Africa who so undoubtedly belonged to that company of elect spirits to whom alone it has been given to reveal the secrets of life.

CHAPTER FOURTEEN
Scoriac Earth

★

THAT farm which I had looked down upon with such excitement from the high crag fulfilled all my anticipations. I was never tired of exploring its more unfrequented areas.

I visited each of the craters in turn. The highest of them rose sharply out of the plain on the other side of the lake. I remember very well the occasion when I first scaled its slopes. I tied Rosinante to a small tree at the foot of a precipitous gully and slowly began the ascent. Half-way up I disturbed some reedbuck. They made a very odd whistling sound and then bounded away, with their white scuts held erect, for all the world like so many chamois, along the shelving ledges. The rocky ground over which I scrambled was covered with a low creeping weed, a weed in appearance not unlike what we call ground-ivy, but possessing an acrid smell, such as one might associate with the sweaty armpit of a leopard. To the right, far above me, the fractured razor-edge of the volcano stabbed its broken outline into the zenith. At last I reached the top of the gully and

actually looked over into the bowl of the crater.
Ten thousand warriors could have camped in that
vast amphitheatre unseen from the plains below.

In the very centre of the hollow circular hill
grew a low tree and under it, perfectly motionless, stood a black object. It was a rhinoceros.
How the heavy beast had ever got into the place
I could not imagine. Two tick-birds were hop-
ping nonchalantly to and fro upon its broad skull.
Its bat's ears were twitching. What was it pon-
dering over down there, as the slow tropical
hours of that particular day slid into eternity?
Was it remembering some far-off season when it
had trotted through the dripping undergrowth at
the square hocks of its mother, or was nothing at
all disturbing its consciousness, nothing except a
drowsy awareness of the grateful circumambient
warmth, and the claws of those eager red-beaked
birds upon the rough surface of its hide? Often
now, when my nerves are distracted, I recall that
scene with a feeling of infinite refreshment. In
vivid retrospection I remember the glaring sunshine, the startling silence of the flat rocks, the
smell of the curious herbage, and the august presence of the somnolent animal. A narrow path,
some few feet wide, ran round the top of the

volcano. Walking on this I was able, not only to see into the bowl, but also cross the plains which lay between its rocky base and the escarpment. I found many traces of rhinoceros even on this dizzy inaccessible ridge; great heaps of dry dung, over which I stepped with difficulty. Down in the plains the zebra appeared like white sea-gulls dotting the green terraces. To the right was a wide expanse of impenetrable country, rock heaped upon rock, boulder heaped upon boulder, a tumbled wilderness stretching as far as the Eburu Mountains thirty miles distant. That savage unshorn acreage remains to-day in precisely the same condition as when the last eruption subsided. It is impossible for human beings to enter its confines. No sooner is one crag surmounted than you are confronted by a second, and each fissure and crevice is overgrown with a dense mat of tangled thorns over which at certain intervals horned cactus-trees wave crooked arms.

The farm encircled this rough country, and in the wet season I would have a sheep-camp pitched near the fig-tree water-hole on its farther side. To reach this camp it was necessary to pass under another crater. One cold early morning as my eyes rested on its giddy heights I noticed that a cloud of white mist was rising into the sky from its topmost ledge. With difficulty I climbed to the place. Through a narrow slit in a rock the mountain was belching steam! A mass of the most amazing hothouse ferns grew there in profusion, presumably nurtured into their extravagant lace-life by the lukewarm moisture. Small wonder, I thought, that the country was insecure, bizarre, seeing that the very crust of the earth itself had hardly settled. Indeed, one felt as if the dazzling, gaudy land, with its striped and spotted creatures, its feathery abnormals, its mammoth vegetation, was sustained by how insubstantial an accident; as if a deep-digging energetic ant-bear might on any moonlit night be the unconscious instrument of bringing about some appalling unprecedented catastrophe!

On the other side of the farm, in the depths of the forest which lay at the foot of the range separating the Rift Valley from Laikipia, was a hot spring. I was particularly fond of frequenting this lonely and lovely place, and would often tie my pony to a neighbouring tree and take off my boots and khaki slacks and red shirt and slip into its steaming waters. The pool was about four feet deep, and if I put my hand behind a

certain stone I could feel the water bubbling up
at a temperature which it was just possible to
bear. I confess that I often felt uneasy bathing
in this pool. It gives one a queer sensation to
be naked and alone in an African jungle. The
mere look of the white skin of a European against
the background of leaves large as elephant's ears
suggests something exotic, out of place. For how
slight, how daintily constructed, how defenceless
is the hairless body of man!

One morning I had gone hardly a hundred
yards from the pool when I heard a sound behind
me and looking round saw the head of an animal
snarling at me from the other side of a bush. I
happened to be leading Ramadan because of the
numerous stones hidden in the long grass. At
first I took the animal to be a particularly savage
hyena until, all at once, I realized that there were
other creatures of the same kind getting up in
the scrub in all directions. I was in no doubt now
as to what they were – a pack of wild hunting
dogs!

Brindled in colour with white about their ears
they kept bobbing up and down in the grass.
They would raise their heads, bare their teeth,
and then once more sink down out of sight. The

stallion did not seem to be in the least disturbed. He snorted and went on as though nothing was the matter. I had no gun with me, not even a stick, only a *kiboko,* or whip, made out of hippo-hide. I did not care for the look of things at all. It seemed to me that an incredible time elapsed before I had led the pony over the few remaining yards of rough ground. Just before I mounted I saw, out of the corner of my eye, that the dogs had gathered in a bunch and were sniff-ing in a puzzled way at the grass over which I had passed, as if uncertain as to the nature of the thing that had disturbed their midday slumbers. There must have been more than twenty in the pack. Once upon Ramadan's back I gave him his head and soon put a safe distance between me and the gully. As a matter of fact I do not think they followed us. I think they had prob-ably killed that morning and had had every intention of sleeping for many more hours in the long grass; but it was no reassuring thought to remember that I had been lolling at ease in the hot pool with these hideous, square-jowled ani-mals enjoying their siesta only a stone's throw away. They are devils, these wild hunting dogs. There is no single animal in Africa which does not hold them in respect. They will even hunt and kill lions if they are hard put to it for food. The imagination of the natives has always been impressed by their ferocity. It strikes them as a most horrible thing to see a buck, black with sweat, flying for its life, and then a moment later to find nothing remaining of it but its horns. When wild dogs come up to the quarry it never touches the ground again. It is tossed about in the air with the pack underneath until there is nothing left. I caught one once in a trap, a very old dog rotten with mange, and its evil look made the worst stories I had heard about them seem credible.

CHAPTER FIFTEEN
Native Women and a Girl
*

THE native women were queer people to look upon. Those belonging to the Masai tribe had their bodies weighed down with heavy bronze rings, so that one wondered how they ever managed to embrace at all. Those belonging to the Kikuyu tribe were covered with a single leather wrap stained with red earth. Some of the young native girls were very attractive, like agile kids with small, delicate, black hoofs. I found it wise to avoid altercation with any of them, especially with the older women. I learned this on the top farm when, on a certain occasion, I tried to prevent a bevy of them walking over some ploughed-up land in search of the peculiar weed, a weed somewhat like chickweed in appearance, which is used by them as a vegetable. Hardly had I stammered out a few words of protest when I found myself the centre of a dozen peevish housewives screaming out incomprehensible words at the tops of their voices. The more angry I grew the louder became the clamour. I could not strike them. I simply could do nothing, and was glad

enough to get out of the way with what sem-
blance of dignity remained to me.

There were always a certain number of un-
attached native women living round the Indian
shops at the station, and these no longer wore
the native dress, but attired themselves instead in
bright-coloured calico drapery, imported into the
country by certain enterprising traders. Asthmani, the old Swahili who looked after the bulls
on the farm, proudly added to his other activities
that of pander. But these old station trots were
by no means engaging companions, and one soon
wearied of seeing them about the place.

Left to themselves the native Africans have
some strange sex customs. For example the
Masai, as long as they are *Il-Muran,* or warriors,
are permitted to live with several maidens of
their tribe, though if any of these girls are got
with child during this period it is regarded as a
grave indiscretion. My boy Kamoha used to tell
me that young Kikuyu boys were privileged on
meeting a girl for the first time to caress her
breasts — a form of salutation which seemed to me
congruous enough with the primeval feline manners of Africa. For the most part, however, the
Kikuyu fathers regard their daughters in the light

of personal property, permission to enjoy their beauty being given only after so many head of goats have been driven into the parental *boma*.

Sometimes of an afternoon I would come to the farm store to find fifty or more Kikuyu women – old women, middle-aged women, young women – each with a big bag of maize for sale, and it would take me till dark to transact business with them. They would often have travelled a hundred miles to earn the few rupees due to them, and occasionally, because I thought they demanded too much, I would refuse to deal and would watch that line of bowed figures winding its way across the plain on its return journey. They carried the grain in bags on their backs, the bags supported by a leather band which encircled their foreheads. I have seen them employ the same method for carrying their babies, the black infant all the time peering out with sharp inquisitive eyes at the strange landscape across which it jogged. Native women are willing to travel without male protection in the daytime, especially if they know that the track they propose taking is not likely to be frequented by baboons. They are terrified of old dog baboons, who, they declare, will often come ambling after them with their squat square buttocks elevated from the ground.

African women are very superstitious, full of inhibitions and taboos of the most curious kind; on the other hand they have no understanding of 'sin' as that hard word is used by Puritans in our Western world. Indeed it is perhaps for this very reason that one grows so soon tired of them, nothing being able to disillusion one more swiftly than a constant ripple of laughter.

I had one adventure with a Kikuyu maiden who could not have been more than sixteen years old. I had ridden far into the forest when suddenly here she was before me, a young native, bending over a water-hole filling a gourd. I reined in my pony. She started with a cry as soon as she saw me. I was the first white man she had seen at such close quarters. I began talking to her in Swahili, but she did not understand a word of that language. However, she soon lost her nervousness, and with the confidence of her sex when they know they are beautiful stood laughing there before me.

She wore a thin strip of leather across her loins. Except for this she was naked. Her brown skin, the colour of an oak-apple, was smeared over with the oil they extract from a eucalyptus-smelling berry. I rode by her side until she reached her hut, a round kraal hidden in a forest glade. I found her father there, busy with his mealie pot. He knew a few words of Swahili and I had some talk with him. After that I rode away. But try as I might I could not get the memory of this forest-child out of my mind. The long, lonely years I had passed in Africa had made my whole being cry out for something to love, for some romance, for it is exactly this that is lacking in the great dark continent.

For several months after this event, whenever I was free in the late afternoon, I would ride up to the forest and stand waiting by the water-hole till Wamboy came. We used to sit side by side under a great forest tree, and I would try to teach her to pronounce certain English words and tease her when her curved lips found difficulty in stammering out the unfamiliar syllables. She was proud and evasive and in every way inaccessible. The sound of her laughter was the prettiest thing I have ever heard in my life. It was clear as the cry of a widgeon on a frosty January morning, clear as the sound of wind in a tall unpollarded poplar-tree. The more I saw of her the more impossible it seemed that I should ever be able to rid myself of the spell she had cast over me. I began to contemplate marrying her. Why not? After all, we have only one life, and surely, I thought, I could spend mine in many worse ways than living in the forest with this lovely creature. I also, like her father, could occupy my time in cultivating a mealie plot, letting all the vulgar importunity of the modern world go to the devil. Other white men had deliberately abandoned civilized life and taken to living with black people; why should not I? I made overtures to the father. He seemed more than agreeable, and told me that if I gave him fifteen goats, ten sheep and one heifer, I could take the girl away whenever I wished. As soon as our plan reached Wamboy's ears she grew frightened. She had been willing to laugh and play, but when she understood that I was really serious a new scared look came into her eyes. It would hardly be true to say that this was altogether unpleasing to me; however, on the whole, it seemed best to avoid meeting her any more. For more than a month therefore I refrained from riding up to our trysting place.

At the end of this time the old man came to

see me. His avarice had evidently been roused. 'Take her,' he said. 'I myself will bring her to you by force any evening you name. When she has lived with you she will come to love you and be no longer frightened.' It was, indeed, a most tantalizing proposal, but the pathos of the girl's alarm and the whole inarticulate grace of her personality made it impossible for me to carry negotiations further. I told the old man to go back to his mealies, and never again looked into the provocative eyes of this rare hamadryad of the African forest.

CHAPTER SIXTEEN
Shears and Fleeces

*

THIS business of looking after fourteen thousand
sheep was no joke. I came to hate these animals,
with their round woolly backs and obstinate selfish
mouths. To prevent scab I was always having to
dip them. At certain intervals they would be put
through a long bath filled with a solution of
Cooper's dip which, when first mixed, was a
bright yellow colour, but later would become a
foul brown. I and two natives stood at the
edge of the channel and with our plungers
pressed the head of each animal under water as it
passed.

The sun would beat down upon us, the dust
from the yard would rise in clouds over the
fences, and the procession of sheep as they clambered up to the dipping pens would seem endless.
Once in the pens the animals would shake themselves, and as I counted them out with the round
yellow sodom-apples, which I used as tallies in
my hands, my nostrils would be filled with the
fumes of the arsenic, sickly warm fumes mixed
with the ammonia which rose from the steaming

brown backs. On such occasions it would seem to me that I was under the influence ·of some strange hypnotic trance, and I would bitterly curse my fate, the miserable monotonous fate of a scurvy shepherd superintending the washing of his flocks.

It was better in the lambing season. This always took place in October, so that the ewes might have the advantage of the fresh grass springing up with the falling of the light autumn rains. I would arrange the lambing camps in different parts of the farm, and pleasant enough it was to come upon these centres of ovine life, with the anxious mothers fitfully nibbling at the creeping grass and the lambs snow-white, long-legged, long-tailed, frisking about on the open veldt. As soon as the lambs were six weeks old I could go from camp to camp ear-marking, castrating, and tailing them. I made a point of doing this in the very early morning, so that the coldness of the air would lessen the bleeding. I became completely hardened to this occupation and would sear off the long appendages of these little symbols of salvation with expert deftness, and as I handled the red-hot copper implement a long thin ray of light would suddenly come slanting

133

across the blood-stained, scorched board at which I worked, and immediately the nervous barking of the impala would cease and the first birds begin to call. When the affair was over I would kneel down and count the lambs by the number of severed tails which lay in a heap at my side, recording the total in my notebook with bloody, sacrificial hands. A dozen or so of the fattest tails I would take back with me, and Kamoha would fry them and serve them up for breakfast like a dish of eels.

In January shearing would begin, and the long rough shed which for the rest of the year remained closed and empty, like a deserted church, would now suddenly become the centre of the farm work. Sheep would baa, natives would chatter, shears would click, the old wool-press would creak, and all would be stir and bustle. It was my business to class the wool, and as fleece after fleece was carried to me I would allocate them to the various bins according to the quality of the staple. There were bins for fleeces, for bellies, for first pieces, for second pieces, and for locks. And the contents of each bin in turn would be baled up and the bales, when they had been stencilled, would be placed on a bullock waggon and hauled to the Uganda railway, to be eventually transported to the London market, there to be ripped open by indifferent merchants, unmindful of the far-distant thickets from which the burs had been caught up, those burs which they so casually noticed deep embedded in the soft crinkled wool.

I would have my breakfast and lunch brought over to the shearing shed and would work there from sunrise to sunset; and often as I stood sharpening the shining knives against the framework of a pen, polished to a rich mahogany brown by countless black fingers greasy from handling sheep, I would look out through the open door and see the wide African country stretching away, mile upon mile, outlandish, unkempt, to where the high mountains rose, upon whose terraces the heavy-limbed marauders slept, their gibbous, gently heaving, obscurely spotted bellies warm in the sun.

And so the long years passed slowly by. I saw little of the neighbouring settlers. My life became reduced to one unending struggle with the material world. To deal with it at all required enormous concentration of energy. My mind alone remained free. That, at any rate, could not become completely subject to an alien domination. Riding along great valleys with a hundred eland before me, riding across wide open clover-grown plains with ostriches zigzagging out of my way, my mind still retained its accustomed detachment.

When I first came to the Rift Valley, Alfred Simpson, an accountant, used to visit me from time to time. He was employed as 'business manager' on a large estate. I used to get very tired of his talk. I have never cared for clerks, and in Africa they seem even less pleasing than elsewhere. He had a pallid face, and one could not look at him without instinctively being reminded of bowler-hats and underground trains. He saved every rupee he could. He put a stop to all petty thieving by keeping his groceries under lock and key. When he had completely worn out his clothes it was his custom to sell them to his natives, and whenever his house-boy broke any of his crockery he had to pay for it. He himself lived extraordinarily poorly, never ate biscuits or canned fruit, in fact anything that cost extra. He neither smoked nor drank. He had been in the country about five years, during which time he had saved enough money to buy himself a coffee farm somewhere near Victoria Nyanza. From certain calculations he made he reckoned to be rich in fifteen years. 'But what are you going to do with this money when you have made it?' I remember asking him. 'Do with it?' he answered in a surprised tone. 'I shall have plenty of things to do with it. I shall go back to London and live well, have plenty to eat and drink and cigars to smoke and a car to drive about in. What do you propose doing yourself?' he asked, by way of a counter-attack. 'Get out of this country as soon as ever I can and find some cottage in the west of England and live there for the rest of my life.' 'Live in a cottage on a hundred a year!' he commented sarcastically. 'Precisely,' I answered. For three years after this conversation I heard practically nothing of him. Once I met a man at the Naivasha Government Sale who came from this district and he told me that Simpson was not very popular with the settlers up there. He never went to see them and when they called gave them water to drink. Meanwhile he starved himself and consistently underpaid the few raw Kavirondo he had working for him. I was interested to hear more of him. He certainly possessed energy and perseverance, and it seemed probable to me that he would get what he wanted.

From the various conversations we had had together I could see his life spread out before me like a map – the long years he had spent in a second-rate boarding-house in London, when, as he told me, he used to sleep so late that he never had time to eat any breakfast, but with the broken dry crumbs of an Osborne biscuit in his mouth and his bootlaces undone would rush off to catch the train for his office; then the few years during which he was possessed by a mania for football, and would exercise himself with his peers on some dreary, obscure playing ground; and finally the unexpected offer of a berth in Africa, which had so entirely changed the normal course of his life.

The last chapter of his story came to me in this manner. I happened to be sitting in one of the low saloons that one comes upon in the back streets of Nairobi, and which are frequented by the rougher element of the Colony, who do not care for the more decorous appearance of the Norfolk Hotel, when a Dutchman, a bulky fellow with a bushy yellow beard, came in drunk. Somehow or another we got talking together, and hearing that he came from the lake, I asked him if he knew anything of my friend. 'Yes, misser,' he said, 'I know Simbson. Simbson vas a great fool. He never eat, he never drink, he say eats and drinks cost money. De dysentery come to his farm and he sends no message. He fears de cost and he dies dere alone on his damned coffee farm, and is now under de ground like all de rest of de damned fools who not eat and drink.'

It was the last word I heard of my acquaintance; but I often find my mind thinking of the poor devil's clerkly bones lying there on that far-off farm while I, by a thousand chances, am still alive to bustle about, blow cigarettes, write choice periods of prose, and eat with sugar upon it the divine red substance of water-melons at each recurring season.

CHAPTER SEVENTEEN
Two African Characters

*

ANOTHER odd character I came across was a
fellow called Fenton. He was a man of about
forty years of age, with red hair and a hatchet-
shaped Scandinavian head. He had taken up
land in the early pioneer days, ploughing the
veldt himself and clearing it of scrub. He had
built a house, a fantastic erection, that stood on
the edge of a deep ravine. It was quite different
from the usual African homestead. It possessed
no fewer than three storeys, and when one saw it
for the first time the incongruity of its appearance struck one with a most unpleasant shock.
The natives were scared to death of Fenton, and
after I had seen his astounding habitation I did
not wonder at it. There was, indeed, something
singularly sinister about the look of this gaunt
rookery stuck up there on the edge of the
jungle.

I did not know the man well. Now and again
I would meet him in a township pub, but as he
was almost always drunk on these occasions our
acquaintance did not progress very fast. A day

came, however, when I was glad enough to accept his hospitality. I had been on a long trek and there was not the ghost of a chance of my reaching home before dark. This depressed me. To tell the truth I never cared much for being out after dark in Africa. It was one of those dismal days in the wet season when the climate of the African plateau undergoes a remarkable transformation and becomes for all the world like the climate of England during October or November. Heavy clouds were drifting across the sky from horizon to horizon, leaving in their track a cold drizzling rain which drenched down upon the trees and upon the rotund backs of the zebra standing under them in melancholy windswept groups. At every step my pony slipped on the soaked ground and little streams of water ran down the saddle, chilling my legs. My rain-coat was simply black with moisture and clung around me sodden and heavy. Even so I think I would have pushed on but for hearing the low grunting of a lion not a quarter of a mile away. It is always unpleasant to find oneself listening to this sound in broad daylight. It means, of course, that the animals are unusually hungry. As I happened to be near the track which led up to

Fenton's house I turned my pony towards it.
Before I reached his door darkness had fallen.

After supper I mentioned the fact that I had
heard a lion down on the plains below. He
answered that there was a man-eater about, and
added that he had been employed in setting a
gun-trap for him that very afternoon.

Before going to bed we stepped out of the
house for a moment. The night was as black as
pitch – no moon, no stars, only one continual
downpour. Suddenly I found myself stumbling
over a number of round slippery objects. They
seemed to be set at intervals along the edge of
the track leading up to my host's front door. I
shouted through the drenching rain to know
what they were. 'Oh, don't go upsetting them,'
came back the answer; 'they are my border.'
'But what are they?' 'Skulls, skulls!' he yelled.
It was perfectly true. The rascal had collected
quantities of these round luminous human bones
and placed them in rows to guide him to his door,
just as in England coast-guards arrange white
stones to show them where the cliff's edge
begins.

The next morning he asked me to come down
with him to the gun-trap. Just as we were start-

ing he was called back to look at a sick cow, and I went on without him. I found the trap quite easily. It was out on the open veldt, some fifty yards from the forest. I approached it with extreme caution, as I always do these circular barricades that so often, for all their harmless appearance, conceal wounded and infuriated animals. I drew closer and closer, but could see nothing. Then I noticed that the lion had broken into the *boma* from the opposite side from where the gun was placed. I felt reassured at seeing this, assuming that the animal had got away unharmed. At last I was able to look into the enclosure. I had expected to see the mangled body of some beast which had been used as bait, the carcass of a bullock or zebra or waterbuck. Instead, lying there before me was the stiff black body of a headless native. That was enough for me. I hurried back and called for my pony. Fenton was vastly amused by my agitation. 'Good God!' he said, 'what's wrong? The man-eater killed the poor devil as he was crossing the stream two days ago and I had nothing else to bait the trap with. But I am certainly sorry that his head has been taken, because I had a place waiting for it at the end of my border!'

The Dutchmen I met in the country were a strange lot. They had come up from the Transvaal, the sons, I take it, of those rough, half-educated backwoodsmen who made the British look so foolish at the time of the Boer War. I could never see any of them without thinking of that melancholy time. I could envisage it all so clearly – the well-disciplined English forces trying to close in upon these sly old foxes of the veldt, who always knew the exact moment to run away and the exact moment to stand dodging behind trees and rocks. The fact is you can never tell what a Dutchman will be up to next. The one I came to know best was employed for several months in making a deep water-hole, or 'tank,' as it would be called in Australia, in an outlying valley of the farm. He lived in a tent on the actual spot, and a wild and undisturbed place it was.

Every few weeks I would ride up to the valley to see how the work was progressing. On these occasions I invariably found him driving his team of oxen backwards and forwards across the pit, emptying, each time before he turned his team, the earth scoop which the oxen were dragging. I would always see him from a long way off, a small figure in a whirlwind of dust, and as I drew nearer I would hear the sound of his shouting and the cracking of his long whip which, with extraordinary dexterity, he used on the flanks of his labouring beasts, that strained and sweated there in the tropical sunshine.

As soon as ever he saw me he would outspan, and we would go together to his tent, where we would sit down and make a meal off something he had shot. I used to enjoy those occasions. I was removed from the worries, the cark and care of the farm, and had only to sit under the grateful shade of the canvas listening to my friend's rambling discourses, and looking out over the dry veldt grass, which, in that burning sunshine, gleamed like a carpet of fine gold.

He was a rough-looking fellow, always half-shaved. Even in his tent he never removed his battered helmet, from under the rim of which sandy-coloured locks of yellow hair protruded. On his feet he wore monstrous boots, boots that looked as heavy as lead, gigantic boots, made out of God only knew what leather, and studded all over with solid pieces of iron, as if they had been horseshoes. I commented one day on their size.

145

'Ach,' he said, 'dose boots are goot boots; a man does not vont dancing boots in dis damn country. Look at de vork I do. I vork hard, Misser Powys.' I was unable to deny this last statement, but still I could not understand his predilection for such weighty footwear. I soon found, however, that he could put them to a good use.

That afternoon he wanted me to go with him to a certain hill-side where he had discovered a spring, the water of which he thought might be sufficient, if properly conserved, for practical purposes. As the place was only three miles away we decided to walk. It was very hot, and as we pushed through the light-coloured scrub the sun kept pricking down upon us with vindictive intensity. I soon began to regret having left my pony behind. The Dutchman's mongrel dog felt the heat as much as we did. Whenever he came to a shady spot where the bush was more than usually thick he would lie down panting, with his hind legs stretched out behind. My friend was very fond of this dog, fond of him with the peculiar tenacious fondness that grows up in the hearts of human beings who live in solitude with only these generous animals as

146

companions. Every time, therefore, that the dog hung back he would insist upon our waiting for him. It seemed to me at this rate we would never reach our destination. Once again we stopped and the Dutchman whistled. We had last seen the dog under a clump of bush a hundred yards behind. Suddenly from that direction we heard an agonized yell. Back we rushed at top speed. As we ran we heard a series of the most pitiful whines, and then to our horror we saw a leopard crouched down with the dog under its paws. Its curved back was turned to us. Evidently it was unaware of our approach. I modified my pace. I did not at all want to have the great brute flying at me. Not so the Dutchman. Without a second's hesitation he rushed up and gave that leopard one of the hardest kicks I have ever seen delivered. His iron-shod boot fairly caught the animal on its firred rib. From where I stood I could hear the dull thud of iron against bone. With a howl of pain the astonished leopard let go its prey and limped off into the bush, doubtless wondering to itself what manner of devil could have given it so diabolic a thump. The dog was badly mauled, but still alive. The Dutchman carried it back in his arms.

'Ach! ach!' he spluttered, 'dat great cat, he dought to eat my poor dog, eh? I vish, Misser Powys, dat he had stayed for me to give him *von more goot booting.*'

CHAPTER EIGHTEEN
The One Righteous Man

*

I USED to enjoy my Sundays in Africa. On these fortunate days I felt myself free to do as I liked. I would sit long over my breakfast, smoking cigarettes while a dozen old cows which were left to graze by themselves near the homestead would hobble after each other towards the water-trough, and the flamingos by the edge of the distant lake would collect in sharp angular groups of flashing colour.

If no news was brought in of untoward accidents, of thieving, or sick cattle, or lost sheep, I would spend the morning reading. I read every line of Shakespeare three times over, I read *Burton's Anatomy of Melancholy,* and every word that Matthew Arnold had ever written. And most restorative I found the long urbane civilized sentences of the latter's prose, prose that kept alive in me the happy knowledge that life contained other concerns than a fretting pre-occupation with material gain. In the afternoon I would go for a walk, up to the forest, or by the side of the stream that wound its way down to

Elmentieta lake. This stream had its source in the hot spring, and for the last mile or so it ran at the bottom of a deep ravine, the tall white chalk-like sides of which were honeycombed with inaccessible caves, the sleeping places of baboons. A rough dam had been constructed across the stream as a reservoir for a small hydraulic ram which pumped water up to the tanks and troughs of the cattle-shed. This small ram-house was reached by a narrow path which had been cut along the precipitous edge of the ravine. I used to take delight in going down this path to sit by the overshadowed pool which gave forth the muddy watery smell of a mill-race at home, that smell which suggests the opening and shutting of the gills of fish, and the breath of eels. I hated the ram. Regularly about once a month it would suddenly stop pumping and somehow or another I would have to get it started again. It would knock and bob and spit, and, indeed, do anything but just continue to give even monotonous beats. It is a dangerous thing for man to try to contend with Nature in Africa. She finds a thousand means to frustrate his purposes. If the mud of the river was not sufficient to choke this ram then a flood would wash away half the stone wall, or little whoreson frogs would get into the pipe, to be squashed to a horrible death against the perforated cylinder.

O Africa! Africa! how eagerly, how savagely, you avenge even so much as the cutting of a branch or the artificial manipulation of a single one of your stones! And yet the hour is fast approaching when even your hard mouth will wince under a hideous double-bit; when even your thick stiff neck will be bowed in ignoble subjection.

Sunday! In Africa it was little enough associated with any religious mood. The tropical sun draws out with its terrible rays all intimations, all suggestions, of that kind of thing, black men and white men alike becoming brutal, soulless, like the spotted beasts. In a land where no rule is recognized but that of rifle, spear and whip, all that is sensitive becomes blighted and crushed down. During the whole of my sojourn there I never had one Christian native working for me. The missionaries confine their efforts to the reserves, only fussing with the boys who surround their particular settlements. No convert ever came my way. Masai, Kikuyu, Nandy, Wakamba, Kavirondo, not one of them had so much as heard of the name of Christ unless, indeed, used with profanity by white lips. One day I 'wrote on' a certain Swahili, an old man whose black woolly hair had already begun to grow white. Swahilis are a coast tribe who for years have had intercourse with Arab traders. They are more useful than the ordinary natives, being more intelligent and more reliable. Since the opening up of the country many of them have drifted into the highlands of the Colony. Salamani was the name of this particular old man, and after he had been with me a month I came to like him extremely. He was slow, but exceedingly honest. I put him to building a cattle-shed, and whenever I rode round that way I always found him hard at work. In fact, I came to regard him as one might some old Dorset labourer who could be trusted. There was one thing about him, however, which used to annoy me. It was a rule on the farm that the day's work should not end until six-thirty, but Salamani, day after day, would go off to his hut at five-forty-five or a few minutes before the sun went down. I used to expostulate with him about this, explaining how bad it was for the other boys to see him leave his work before the appointed time. On such occasions he would give me to understand that he had taken in what I said, yet the very next day there he would be shuffling off in the direction of his hut the same as ever. It happened that I was particularly anxious that the shed should be finished as soon as possible so that I could house some animals in it. It was Salamani's business to thatch the roof with certain long feathered reeds which grew in the swamps near the lake. Imagine then my exasperation one late afternoon at finding the whole work at a standstill because, as the other natives were at pains to explain to me, Salamani, who alone was able to lay the straw correctly, had considered it the moment to knock off. Speechless with indignation I went over to his hut, which stood by itself on a sloping hillock overlooking the lake. As I drew near I walked quietly, *kiboko* in hand, intending to take him by surprise and teach him once for all that he could not leave work just as his will prompted.

On reaching the back of his hut, where a row of shining 'debbies' stood, I was conscious of hearing a strange mumbling sound. I crept round, and there in front of his house I saw him. But I could not raise my hand. There was something about his attitude which entirely disarmed me. Salamani was praying.

There he was, on his knees, his arms raised high above his white poll. There he was, praying, as his fathers had been taught to do by the Arab traders of long ago, who themselves had been taught by their fathers, who years back had been taught by the Prophet himself. Silently I retraced my steps. Now I knew that on this remote Rift Valley farm where we lived lives devoid of love, devoid of religion, there yet remained one human being who night and morning never forgot to supplicate the Deity at the rising and the setting of the sun.

Although it is true that the natives do not worry their heads much about God, they have a kind of morality of their own, a sense as to fitness of behaviour. I once sold three half-bred cows which had just calved to a white dairyman. I had ridden up to his farm, and when we had come to an agreement as to the price he asked me into his house to drink to the success of the transaction. I shall never forget entering his little front room. It was as if an English dairyman's cottage had been transported into the heart of Africa. There was the solid horsehair arm-chair opposite the fire-place, the half-dozen ordinary chairs straight and stiff and covered with cheap varnish, the rug made of little tags down by the fender, the commonplace pictures of rural scenes, villainous to look at, and each of them with its church tower showing across complacent meadows. Over the chimney (and this arrested my attention more than anything) were photographs of his mother and father, photographs enlarged so that the shadowy faces of these simple people were almost life-size. I looked at them. The old man wore side whiskers, and his physiognomy expressed that particular combination of kindly stupidity and shrewd honesty which is so typically English. The old lady, in her white cap, gave one the impression of utter contentment, so that as one looked at her and at the old man one began almost to fancy that the world from which they sprang must in reality be all that they considered it to be – a place well ordered and decorous, a place of steady and placid work, where bells rang out for church once every week, and where the seasons followed each other for seventy years in undeviating regularity, the swallows and spring flowers giving place to hay-making and the sweating heat of an English midsummer, followed in

its turn by cider-making and the long months
when the cattle were kept in the barton, each of
them with a shining chain round its neck, and
fed on hay and as much cake as would ensure no
decrease in the amount of milk they were giving.

I sent the three half-breds to the dairyman's
farm a few days later, under the care of a Masai
called Lesolio. On his return I asked him about
his visit. For some time he was silent and then
he said, 'Is it the custom among white men to
starve their stock to death?' and with the quaint-
est gestures he began to re-enact what he had
seen.

The dairyman, overjoyed at the sight of the
heavy udders of the cows he had bought, had
tied them up and milked them at once. 'Now,
at last I shall have enough milk for my cheeses,'
he had thought. It was not, therefore, until he
had extracted nearly all of the precious white
liquid that he found it in his heart to allow the
calves to suck, and even then, so I understood
from the mimicry of the black man, he still kept
hold of their hind quarters, pulling them away as
soon as he thought they had had enough. True
tradesman that he was, he did not wish a pint
more milk to find its way into the stomachs of

the calves than was necessary to keep them alive.

To Lesolio his action had appeared both cruel and incomprehensible. The Masai could not understand that if the price of cheese was relatively higher than the price of cattle, the man considered he was doing a perfectly legitimate and rational thing in starving the calves. To the primitive mind of the native no transitory economic conditions could possibly justify so mean an outrage upon the ancient laws of nature. In fact, this deliberate starving of young animal life in order to make white cakes was, in his sight, nothing but a horrible blasphemy.

'*Mzungu sasa fisi, baya sana*' ('That white man is like a hyena, very bad. He must be like the Wandorobo and have forgotten altogether the words that his father used to speak to him over the camp-fire').

CHAPTER NINETEEN
Food for Cannibals
*

DAY followed day, month followed month, and still I saw no hope of release. The war continued. It seemed to me that it would never end. The Colonial Government presently began to commandeer carriers for the campaign in German East Africa. The death-rate amongst these human beasts of burden was terribly high. I had already heard rumours of it, and I confess that when the District Commissioner asked me to hand over twelve boys I was in no happy mood. One of the twelve I selected was a native called Korombo. He was a Kikuyu, but he differed from other boys of his tribe in that he was extremely fat. Indeed, without exception, he was the fattest native I have ever come across. He resembled one of those obese youthful monstrosities that one notices from time to time walking about in the New York streets. Great rolls of flesh could be seen under his blanket, and his legs were so well covered that it was impossible to see the bones of his knees.

Korombo accepted my decision with the characteristic fatalism of his race. Muúngu (God) had caused this protracted fight amongst the white men; Muúngu had arranged that the official should write to me; Muúngu had put it into my head to select him, Korombo, as one of the twelve to be sacrificed.

Before leaving, he brought me a native sheep, requesting that it should be kept for him till his return. It was as absurd to look at as its master, covered with hair instead of wool, and fat as a porpoise. I put it in a flock of half-bred wethers.

A year passed without any news of Korombo. Meanwhile the most ghastly stories kept leaking out concerning the shameful mismanagement of the carrier corps. The mortality among them was appalling. Thousands upon thousands were dying. Each time I counted the half-bred wethers I was reminded of Korombo. My eye would suddenly notice his grotesque animal and I would wonder to myself what had become of its owner, that friendly plump negro who had been so arbitrarily chosen by me 'to do his bit.'

A second year passed, and then one evening, just as I was putting my key into the lock of the store, whom should I find standing by my side but Korombo himself! He was in high feather.

He had obtained his discharge the week before
in Nairobi and was once more free. He was full
of stories of his adventures, and as I sat with him
and a number of other natives over the fire that
the herders used to keep going between the store
and the stockyard fence, this side of the small
gate, I listened with absorbed interest to the
various impressions that had penetrated to the
brain of this corpulent savage during his sojourn
in German East Africa.

The food, he declared, had been abominable,
and he indicated with his cupped hand the exact
size of the wretched portion of rice which had
been allowed him for each day; the work had
been heart-breaking, and he got up and imitated
the laborious motions of an over-burdened human
body. But this had not been all. There had been
other things calculated to make him feel ill at
ease. Apparently the Belgians had enlisted in
their battalions a great number of cannibal tribes-
men from the far interior of the Congo. Korombo,
of course, was fighting on the same side as these
jolly Rogers, but, as he explained with a wry
smile on his black face, he did not feel very nice
when troops of this kind were quartered near by.
He had happened upon them once, he told me,

in the streets of a small village. They were marching along in disciplined order when suddenly they caught sight of his well-conditioned body. Immediately they began grinning at each other and calling out *'Nyama! Nyama!'* ('Meat! Meat!') 'That was not very pleasant for me,' he said; 'I felt just exactly as my fine sheep will tomorrow when I take him out of the flock, *for those jackals were hungry I tell you.'*

CHAPTER TWENTY
Paul J. Rainey and Others

★

I<small>T</small> is strange how clearly I remember certain well-known East African characters, how well I can recall the very tones of their voices, their gestures, their habits, the very words that issued out of their mouths!

I recollect Paul J. Rainey, and can see him now returning from a successful lion hunt along the track which ran below the escarpment, can see him returning astride his pony, in all the vigour of his prime, good-natured, insensitive, and with his mind as innocent of thought as any of the animals he hunted. We had started out early that morning and had reached the edge of the lake before the sun rose. The hounds put up nothing in the rushes except two golden-crested cranes that went sailing away overhead uttering their quavering haunted cries as if their two outstretched feathered bodies imprisoned the dolorous souls of an impassioned Pharaoh and his leman, long since dead. The sand on which my pony stood was crisp and ribbed with soda, and everywhere its crust had been cracked and broken by the heavy footfalls of the self-absorbed hippo-potami which had returned but lately to their watery retreat.

From the lake we crossed an open plain. The sun had just risen, and a beauty cool and trans-lucent had fallen for a moment across the hag-gard features of the Equatorial landscape. A hundred yards away stood a herd of zebra, their sleek striped flanks and inquisitive mottled heads in perfect harmony with the dazzling scene, with the dew-bespangled foreground, with the yellow spiked trees, and with the gleaming silver reaches of the lake. Paul J. Rainey looked at them. 'I would like,' he said, 'to send a bullet into that little outfit.' In the next valley the hounds got upon the scent of a lion. 'I sees you, I sees you, you son of a bitch.' Thus and not otherwise did the coke millionaire address the King of the Forest.

The highest form of happiness that Paul J. Rainey was capable of experiencing was in its essence identical with that of the simplest farm boy, whose joy it is to dig out badgers in a mid-night copse. To Paul J. Rainey the whole world represented a midnight, moonlit copse. Because his father had happened to be a lucky speculator there was scarcely a portion of the earth's surface where wild animals were safe from his depredations. In Africa he once killed nine lions in thirty-five minutes. In the Arctic regions an incredible number of polar bears, walruses, and seals fell to his gun, without counting the animals that he brought back in cages. And like a half-educated farm boy I do not suppose that once during the whole forty-six years of his consciousness he felt the slightest misgiving for the havoc that his presence brought to the wild life of the countries he visited. The lions of Kenya Colony, distracted by so many dogs at their heels, were soon 'brought up in short order,' to use Mr. Rainey's own favourite expression. A selfish man, a superficial man, a commonplace man, he was, still, if I am not much mistaken, haunted all his years by something wild and beautiful in the varied life he loved so much to destroy.

Did he, one wonders, on that last September day, before he in his turn was 'brought up in short order' as he sailed towards the Cape, recollect, with that curious vividness which impending disaster will sometimes give to the memory, the frozen loon-crowded ledges of Cape York which overlook that vast white acreage belonging to the top of the world, the whispering cane-brakes of the Mississippi, the black pools, papyrus-shaded, which lay near his Naivasha farm? It may well have been so. One of his most delightful characteristics was the affection he felt for his hounds, that deep intimate affection that is one of the paradoxes of the sportsman's nature. I can still hear his voice, that powerful, deep-lunged American voice, cheering on his hound, 'Ring,' as we drew near to a lion at bay in one of the glades of the Karianduce Valley.

Paul J. Rainey was buried at sea somewhere between Southampton and the Cape of Good Hope on the 18th of September, 1923, which was the forty-sixth anniversary of his birthday.

Perhaps it will be best to refer to some other East African celebrities in a more guarded fashion.

A—(who should know him if not I?) was like one of the hawks whose cry was such music for his ears as they swept by, far up over the rocky escarpments. He confessed to me once that the two sounds in Africa he loved most were the wild whistle of this bird and the moaning of the wind through the ant-eaten thorn bushes of the Laikipia plains. And well he might love these sounds, for most strangely were they in harmony with his proud, dark nature, which bowed itself before neither man nor God.

I once caught an eagle in a rat gin, and the haughty glance it gave me out of its yellow-rimmed eye (its wings had been bound together with strips of bark) was identical with the glance of my friend when he felt Fate's evil clutch upon him. The astonished natives explained the mysterious dynamic power of his personality by simply asserting that 'he had a black stomach.' And truly the man was stark; but for all this he loved a good round-nosed ram as though it had been his father. How I used to like to see him fumbling amongst his sheep, his deft muscular hands covered with tar!

And yet if he could be assured that his flocks were in his pens, that his cattle were in his yards, that his bulls were in his sheds, that all was well with his horses, that his hay was under cover, that his lucerne was well watered, that his silo-pit was the right temperature, that none of his rupees was like to be stolen from his safe of triple brass, then no intellectual conception was too subtle or too delicate for him to appreciate. His was a witty intellect free from cant, and many were the quips he would let fly when there was a good bundle of crackling olive wood on the hearth. Yet on his very death-bed the mere suspicion that one of his mules was being galled on its withers by the carelessness of an ignorant manager would put him into a passion. The divine art of fireside conversation, of poetry, of philosophy, was in his opinion merely a charming accessory to life, to the serious, all-important occupation of raising fat wethers for the market. As is so often the case with distinguished people, his face seldom appeared the same. I have sat spell-bound before the unconscious nobility of his head, that head with its high white forehead, its proud sensitive nose, its clear firm eyes. These were on occasions when his bulls were safely housed and his sheep safely penned. At other times, perhaps when he was rating some wretched underling, his wry twisted mouth so completely disfigured the rest of his countenance as to give the impression of something as sour to the taste as the wrinkled skin of a withered crab-apple. But again there would anon pass over his face a look as gentle and sensitive as that of a young girl, and such a look in the darkest hour of my misery would never fail to win me back to his service. He was indeed a man, taking him all in all. God with

His clumsy grip can break his back, but never his spirit. Haughty, arrogant, reckless, magnanimous, it goes to its doom asking no mercy.

B— was another character I admired. He could best be likened to a sinuous-limbed dog-puma indolently sunning himself under the swaying palm-trees of the Amazon till such a time as vigorous action is imperative. One got the impression that he could bring anything he undertook to a fortunate issue. He had the same quality of courage as A—, but was far less reckless, combining the audacity of some old-time Elizabethan with the wisdom and foresight of the son of Laertes. I saw him first fingering a pistol in a Nairobi gun-shop, fingering it with the casual interest that men of action will show for such toys, and well I liked the look of his scholarly appearance, which had also about it the suggestion of an adventurous wanderer, of a man who knew every hidden creek and broad reach of the Upper Nile, and who had watched a hundred desert suns splash with gilt the white-walled cities of Somaliland.

C— resembled exactly one of those pouting, short-legged, round breast-boned, self-important, red-cheeked Chinese geese I used to like to watch

in the Botanical Gardens at Cambridge. I can
see them now complacently strutting at the edge
of the shallow artificial lake, emitting every few
empty seconds, cackles at the blue sky above their
heads. Was C– superficial out of profundity?
Had he taken stock of life and in consequence
concluded that 'twere best to be content with the
appearance of things – with the applause, in fact,
of a set of second-rate land speculators? Where
was his soul hidden, that little, vain, spry soul
that no man has ever seen? What a flow of
talk, of wit even, could emerge from his small
voluble mouth! On one occasion he picked up
a slim volume of the poems of William Barnes
on my table. It was, as a matter of fact, that
much-cherished selection that Thomas Hardy
made some years ago. 'Probably the man spent
his whole life writing that book,' he said con-
temptuously; in that single exclamation exposing
once and for all the essential Philistinism of his
mind.

Miss D– used to sell me some of her second-
best lettuces. In any station of life she would
have been a character, and a distinguished character. Exiled in Africa she had allowed her pre-
datory impulses to assume enormous proportions.

It became an obsession with her to prevent the smallest leakage in her budget. She suffered pain if one of those queer African rats, striped like a zebra, nibbled at a single grain of her chicken-food. She reminded one of a brooding hen of the highest pedigree who had been turned off its nest by my lord's footman. If mortals were subject to a moral discipline from above she should be compelled with her own hands to throw a golden guinea away every morning before she said her prayers.

E– was an important Government official, a gross sottish old man who drank a prodigious amount of whisky and reminded one of an ill-favoured and ancient walrus who had become debased by long years of ease in captivity. He treated his subordinates in the heartless manner of a man unused to authority, and for recreation diverted his mind by reading second-rate magazines.

Lord Ding Dong had, it is true, two or three great honey-bees humming under his helmet. Without doubt he was the kindest and the most truly religious man to be found in the colony. Albeit his round head was packed to the brim with nice theological whimseys he had a most liberal spirit. At every hour of the day he would cry to his God: when he was having his cold bath, when he was galloping like a trooper over the plains after some poor devil of a hyena, or when he sat at the side of some dying man. And who can tell but that the simple thoughts of this most pious and most just Ding Dong came nearer to the truth than those of the more sophisticated! Perhaps all these greedy, vulgar, white settlers, all these hapless, casual negroes, all these savage and sly animals, these hungry birds, and vain flowers of the mid-African plateau were in very truth under the scrupulous scrutiny of a hallowed eye, which remained for ever unhooded somewhere far up above the craters, above the sun-warmed back of the highest vulture poised aslant in the radiant levels of the planet's upper air.

CHAPTER TWENTY-ONE
Drought

*

THE last year of my stay in Africa was terrible. Famine stalked through the land with Pestilence galling his kibe. Week after week the country lay prostrate under the blank stare of a soulless sun. Month after month the waters of the lake sank lower and lower. Its lagoons and shallows dried up, and each night a gusty burning wind carried across the veldt the poisoned sulphuric exhalations of its wide muddy reaches. It was as though the earth itself were undergoing some appalling process of putrefaction. The air was tainted, the flaked dusty mould stank. The buck no longer frolicked on the plains, but either trekked in long lines from horizon to horizon or congregated about the few streams where water still ran. Everywhere one came across the carcasses of animals dead from exhaustion, carcasses with long muddy tongues protruding, as though the wretched beasts up till the very last moment had hoped to suck in moisture. The vultures grew plump as Michaelmas geese. And still no cloud, no veil of mist ever appeared in the sky. The sun rose and sank in a blinding heaven, and under its hideous presence all sensitive life trembled and shrank. The lions and leopards lay up near the few befouled water-holes and, because the haunches of their victims were lean, killed the more often. As I rode through the forest I came upon gazelles from the plains searching nervously in an alien environment for cool retreats. Enormous coiling serpents battened upon their thirsty frightened bodies. Monkeys came down from the tree-tops and in wavering processions went looking for new watering-places.

The crops never came up. The Government imported large quantities of grain from the South, but even so, a great many natives died of starvation. I used to see troops of them moving along the old caravan road, supported by the pathetic illusion that they would at length come to some fat land where there would be enough food for all. It was useless to tell them that their quest was hopeless. They would not listen, but continued to journey on, day after day, in trailing ant-like lines – tall men, women with milkless breasts, and little dazed, wrinkled children. My work, of course, became much harder throughout this time. I had often considerable difficulty in getting enough meal for the actual requirements of the farm. The authorities kept postponing their consignments, and although I never actually ran out, yet I often experienced periods of considerable anxiety. Stealing of every kind increased. Sheep camps were raided by native robbers, one night five ewes being taken out of the home yards, under my very nose. In this case I suspected the herder of being in league with the thief and made what investigations I could. My suspicions eventually rested on a native called Kapingy, who was a squatter in the forest with six children to support. I was particularly exasperated, because I had done all that I could to help him, giving him every week an allowance of meal sufficient in quantity to keep him and his family till the evil time should come to an end.

I had felt sorry for the fellow. I knew him to be as hard-working as natives ever are, and I had noticed on his face that harassed, preoccupied look which comes to men, black, yellow, and white, when they have children dependent upon them and cannot find enough food to keep them alive.

174

This feeling now turned to indignation. 'What a sly devil!' I thought. 'Just like all the rest of these people who have black hides: every time you are generous to them you are certain to be overreached.'

I made up my mind to catch him out by making a raid upon his hut. I let the affair slide for three days so that he should consider himself safe, and then one afternoon rode up to his forest home. As I came near the place I smelled very distinctly the odour of roasting flesh. Dismounting, I crawled through the low door into his darkened kraal. A huge cauldron was on the fire and round it sat Kapingy and his six starving children. I was certainly shocked to see how thin they all were. The flickering light illumined their bodies, bringing out into horrible relief first a rib bone, then a collar bone, then a hip bone. '*Jambo Bwana!*' said Kapingy, as though he was glad to see me. ('Ah,' I thought, 'he is pulling wool over my eyes. He thinks to fool me like this, hoping that I won't look into his pot.') '*Jambo Kapingy!*' I answered, and seizing two sticks I lifted out of the steaming saucepan the skinny body of a starved wood-rat!

With only one small permanent stream on the

farm the stock became terribly congested. The tracks down to the various watering-places had for weeks been reduced to bare dusty wastes, upon which not a blade of grass was to be seen. When the famished panting flocks came to these arid places they would know they were near water, and animated once more would emit strange treble baas and scamper pell-mell down the last decline. Some of the flocks came from camps several miles distant, and one could follow the course of their return journey by the clouds of grey dust which rose above their backs into the palpitating air. It was wonderful to me how they kept alive at all, subsisting apparently upon nothing but water and dry grass stalks.

As the weeks passed the great lake itself fermented. The hippopotami grew fastidious, and, leaving their bubbling fetid resting-places, would come floundering up the river bed to slake their thirst with purer water. One old bull actually left the river and took to drinking from a farm trough. This trough was made of tin sheets. I would not have objected in the least to his drinking from it, if only he had done so with care and decency. As it was, he must put his great hoofs in the trough and bend and crush it to pieces in an endeavour to get a greater flow of water. I sat up for him one night, but although I had a shot at his bulging body he got back to the lake, plunging into the black expanse with an enormous splash. I could see the gap where it was his custom to come through the fence which surrounded the trough; so I constructed a framework of tall poles and set a gun-trap over it. I found it tiresome, however, having to unset and reset this contrivance every morning and evening, though it was a labour I could not neglect with so much stock about; but I had no sooner decided to remove it, when a native came flying in to say that a hippopotamus of a stupendous size had been shot and was lying at the lake's edge. I mounted my pony and rode to the place. The hippopotamus was indeed of extraordinary proportions, like a whale, like two elephants in one. I had often noticed colossal hippo tracks in the sand of the lake's margin, which I now concluded must have belonged to this animal, to this father of all hippopotami.

I cantered towards it. As I came nearer, its size seemed to increase rather than diminish. Its bulk was beyond anything I had conceived possible in the animal world – beyond anything I had ever read about. It was not until I was within a few yards of it that I became suspicious. The wind was not my way, but even so the air was foul. The explanation flashed upon me. This was none other than the hippopotamus I had shot at a fortnight ago. I had evidently mortally wounded it, and now, swollen like a balloon from decomposition, it had floated in here. I told a Kikuyu, a boy named Korogo, to get the ivory. I gave him an axe and instructed him somehow or another to chop it out of the beast's head. He brought it to me in the evening, declaring that he wanted the heaviest recompense for his labour. I gave him what he asked. I had not forgotten the glimpse I had of that mass of corrupting matter, with its huge four feet turned white.

One day an old Masai told me that long before the coming of the white men he remembered his father telling him that there was water at the end of a certain cave in a distant valley. He told me it had never been used because everybody feared going in to the place, seeing that at the end of it there lived *an evil thing*. I pricked up my ears at once. It would be wonderful to have a water

supply in that arid portion of the farm. I knew
the cave to which he referred. I had come upon
it once when out shooting guinea-fowl. I also was
sufficiently acquainted with geology to realize
that it must have been formed by water at one
time or other. I determined to investigate; and
the next day, taking with me a large blizzard-
lantern, I rode up to the spot. The cave lay at
the bottom of a deep pit, the sides of which were
overgrown with fig-trees and other bushes. I tied
up my pony and with some difficulty clambered
down to its mouth. This was about four feet
high. I lit my lantern and entered. Once within,
I found myself in a large cavernous room, a room
paved with vast boulders which had evidently
fallen from the roof. Some of the boulders were
so large that it was difficult to get round them.
The breath of the place was as the breath of a
tomb. I did not like the look of things at all,
and as I made my way forward I kept turning
my head in the direction of the doorway, through
which I could still see a glimmering ray of light.
I was not afraid of meeting a wild animal in the
place. It seemed to me unlikely that any beast
would select so cold a lair; but I was apprehensive lest the rocks from the roof should either

come down upon me or, what seemed even worse, obstruct in their collapse my passage out. It was no wish of mine to be entombed for ever in the bowels of Africa.

It was certainly an astounding tunnel, and it apparently went on for ever. I was reminded of the legendary entrances into hell. Presently, on looking back, I no longer saw light from the cave's mouth. I still went forward however, picking my way amongst the rocks and stones as best I could. The light from my lantern irradiated vast slabs above my head, slabs of stone so smooth and flat that one could hardly believe that they had not been polished by human hands. From some of them I saw bats hanging, bats large as blackbirds, with leathery wings closed tight round their bodies. Suddenly I heard a noise and realized that something was beating up in my direction. I held my pistol ready, but I was extremely reluctant to shoot, for I feared that the concussion might cause some of the rocks to fall. A second later I was reassured as a large white owl flapped its way past me.

Again I advanced, holding my lantern high and peering into the darkness ahead. Its light fell upon something leaning against one of the walls, something that quite obviously was neither rock nor stone. A chill dread held me in suspense. What in God's name was this muffled shadow standing so silently there? Was I, after all, not by myself in the cave? Was there someone else with me, someone at that very moment standing mute at my elbow? I put out my hand and touched it. I examined it closely. It was the skeleton of a large buck. The horns, though discoloured, were in good condition and the bones were still encased in a hide which was stretched over them like tight parchment. Behind the buck lay the dust-covered form of another animal. I cannot tell why, but there was something horrible to me about finding these remains in this silent geological chasm. I turned and with all possible expedition got myself out. How had they come there, I wondered – how and when? What terror had driven that sun-loving animal to take refuge in so strange a place, and when the hyena followed, what dread subterranean miasma had stricken them both dead? Had they been there for a hundred, for a thousand years? Doubtless to this hour they are there, sepulchred in the silent belly of Africa. The cave is situated under the crater with the steam jet, the crater which I used to call 'High,' not far from the group of trees beneath which in the rainy season the eland and grant like to assemble.

CHAPTER TWENTY-TWO
Writing in the Dust

★

THE grass had now become so scarce on the plains that the herders had each day to drive the cattle up to certain hidden glades near the hot springs, where they could feed knee-deep in rough, dry herbage. Conditions were better in these forest openings. The foliage of the trees was still green here, whereas in the lowlands the narrow silver leaves of the lilishwa bushes had for months been dangling limply from their twisted twigs. The one thing I dreaded was a forest fire. In these deep-wooded dells what hope would I have of extinguishing any such conflagration? Imagine then my dismay one late afternoon at actually seeing a puff of smoke rise from the top of the escarpment which overhung the forest. Well I knew what the presence of that tiny uncertain wisp of smoke would mean in a few hours' time. Galloping back to the homestead I collected every native I could and sent them off to try to beat it out. Already, fifteen minutes after I had seen that first slender pillar against the sky, great billowing clouds of smoke were floating across the

Rift Valley. One smelt smoke in every breath, and the light from the sinking sun was obscured.

By the time I was ready to set out myself darkness had fallen. The dome of heaven was splashed with a bloody glare. From the door of my hut, with my foot in the stirrup, I could see the outline of the flames. The cattle were lowing in the yards, and a feeling of universal uneasiness was upon man and beast. It seemed sometimes, as one burst of flame succeeded another, as though the sheds and huts and yards were about to be consumed, as though this whole section of Africa was about to go up in flames.

The best way on to the escarpment lay some five miles distant, but I knew of a certain game-path which zigzagged up its precipitous side from a much nearer point. I hesitated for a moment; but as I was anxious to reach the fire, and had often ridden that way in the daytime, I decided to take it now. All went well at first. Rosinante seemed to know each turn and our advance was rapid. To reach the top of the escarpment it was necessary to scale a succession of high forest terraces, consisting of level spaces of jungle some few hundred yards wide, and divided each from the other by rocky cliffs, up which the narrow circuitous path crept. Whenever the pathway became too rough or too steep I would get off my pony and lead him. I had reached the last of these terraces, and could already hear the boys shouting as they fought with the flames, when an unpleasant thing happened. Somehow or another I must have taken a wrong turning, because I found myself pushing through virgin undergrowth. I tried to retrace my steps, but go where I might I could not recover my bearings. Eventually I sat down on a fallen tree, exhausted and out of breath. It was then, as I rested shut away by myself amongst those dark tree-trunks, that I realized the ghastly nature of my predicament. In a moment I was on my feet. What a fool I had been not to have understood before that unless I could find my way out of the forest I might very well be burnt alive!

Dragging Rosinante after me I rushed this way and that. Continually we were brought up short by impenetrable barriers, by masses of thorny jasmine, by fallen trees piled one upon the other, the accumulated legacy of long-forgotten centuries. After desperate attempts to force my way through or over these obstructions I would be driven back

on my tracks, only to find myself even more
hopelessly lost. In that vast confusion of vegetable growth it seemed impossible that I should
ever find the small game-path again. I may have
crossed and recrossed it a dozen times for aught
I know. I followed countless false tracks, only
to be disappointed. Some of them led me to the
very edge of the cliff that separated me from the
terrace beneath. Looking over a sheer drop of
a hundred feet I would see below a shadowy
undulating surface of tree-tops that seemed to
extend for ever. Why had I not been more pru-
dent? I had been betrayed by that sense of false
security that life under civilized conditions nur-
tures; had taken it for granted, so to speak, that
one could not be trapped by a bush-fire. I tried
to collect my thoughts, to keep cool, and consider
what was the right, the intelligent thing to do
under circumstances of this kind. Climb a tree?
No, the tree itself would catch fire. What then?
Creep into some rocky cleft and trust that I
would not be suffocated. But what about Rosinante? I could not abandon him. Already scarlet
sparks were flying overhead like a host of red
locusts, like fireflies. I could see them far up
through the branches. I could hear the shouts of

the boys as they fought with the flames – *'Uwee!
Uwee! Uwee!'*

I called, I yelled, but my voice thinned to a
faint echo, drowned by another sound, a mumbling maniacal sound which every second grew
louder and louder – the hungry eager reverberation of oncoming flames.

Suddenly something crashed through the forest
a few yards to my right – a rhinoceros! Desperately I followed along the pathway it had made.
My impulse was right. I had to go only a short
distance when I found myself at the top of the
path up which I had come. In half-an-hour I was
safely out on the plains. Before midnight the
forest was a burning furnace. The boys had had
to retreat and retreat before the fire, and we only
stopped its advance on the dusty levels across the
river. A wind had risen, and even on ground
practically denuded of grass it was no easy thing
to put the flames out. It was as though the actual
dust had been soaked with paraffin, so eagerly
did the red tongues leap from tuft to tuft.

I was up all that night. As soon as we had
burnt fire-breaks between the escarpment and the
farm it was necessary to forestall the fire's advance
towards the forest on the other side of the hot

spring where the native squatters lived. I rode
from one strategic position to another directing
operations, a frightened and excitable Napoleon
on a white pony. The forest to the left now
appeared like a lamplit city – like Brighton as I
have looked down upon it at night-time from
some high shoulder of the South Downs. The
red-hot branches of certain dead trees outlined
themselves against the darkness as though a
hundred flaming crucifixes had done to death a
hundred gods. The river banks, the water-holes,
the mud paths, the stones, were aglow with a
strange ecliptic light, and from time to time, as
I directed my pony through this sinister haze,
scared shadows would cross my path migrating
to unburnt country.

The white light of dawn was already visible
when at last I reached my hut. I went to bed,
giving instructions to Kamoha not to let anybody
disturb me. It was noon when I woke. A native
from a distant sheep camp was at my door. He
had come to say that a herder called Merishu
was sick, sick with some horrible sickness which
he suggested I very possibly knew nothing about.
I promised to ride to the camp as soon as ever
I had breakfasted. In Africa one agitation will

often follow so close upon another that one grows dizzy, and one's very sensibility becomes dull. This Merishu was a favourite boy of mine. I always remember the first time I set eyes on him. It was in October, and he came striding towards my house, spear in hand, a very picturesque figure against the crimson aloes which are always in flower at that season of the year. Alone of all the Masai I have ever met he was not indifferent to Europeans and their ways. He would listen with grave attention to anything that I might tell him about England. He was especially impressed, I remember, by two facts – namely, that sheep and cattle could be left out at night by themselves; and that girls could not be sold by their fathers. It used to fascinate him to see me write in my sheepman's notebook, and he begged me to teach him 'to speak on paper' in the same way. I presented him, therefore, with a book and a pencil, and copied out as clearly as I could all the letters and numerals. After this, whenever I went to see how his sheep were getting on, he would produce his exercise and with the utmost pride show me the rude symbols he had managed to trace each night over the camp-fire. He was the only native I ever knew who paid the slightest attention to writing; as a rule they seem to regard it as a kind of witchcraft entirely removed from them and their affairs.

I rode up to his camp as soon as I could. He lived in the half-section of a corrugated iron water-tank. The tank had been too old to use for its original purpose, so I had divided it into two halves, each of which made a satisfactory and portable shelter. As soon as I came near this queer shell-like habitation I called to Merishu by name. He crawled out. I saw at once what was the matter – he was suffering from smallpox. I gave him some salts to drink and some oil to rub over his body, and found a boy of his own tribe to look after him. The next day I was too busy to get back there, and the day following there was a slight recrudescence of the fire which kept me occupied. When I returned on the third day his situation had indeed become terrible. The boy I had sent to look after him had, in true native fashion, run away. How long Merishu had been by himself I could not tell. His condition was dolorous. There was not a portion of the surface of his body uncovered with little round hideous eruptions. They were on his face, his back, his penis, the very soles of his feet. He lay in the dust dumb as a serpent, indicating by a terrible look and feeble gestures that he wanted water. I went and fetched some and put it on the ground before him. Dragging himself on to his elbow, he began lapping at it like an animal. He finished it and sank back. Then it was I noticed that one of his hands was feeling about for something, and in a little while it took up a thin pen-like tally-stick and began tracing hieroglyphics in the dry mud. When he had finished he looked up with a heartrending expression, as though to implore me somehow or another to construe a meaning from his crude symbols. Of course I could not make head or tail of them. Did they refer to some delirious anxiety with regard to the welfare of his sheep, or had they to do with the place where his savings were buried, or was he making a last desperate attempt to communicate something of his forlorn isolation in that terrible hour?

I went away to secure another boy to look after him, but when we got back he was dead. He was lying on his side, his head resting on his indecipherable alphas and omegas, while his pimply cusped hand was still grasping the thin stick that had served him for a pen.

The next day I cremated his body. I had a cartload of firewood hauled to within a few yards of the tank and then, as I could get no natives to help me, slowly built up a funeral pyre. There in the centre of a wide plain, with the sun so directly above my head that my form cast no shadow, I burned the man, heaping the wood higher and ever higher, till his thigh bones protruded and his scorched flesh fell away.

CHAPTER TWENTY-THREE
Black Laughter

*

IT was at this time that I experienced one of the strangest of all my African adventures, the very recollection of which I still find obscure and bewildering. It was as though in that remote corner of the world I received a sinister hint as to the existence of certain influences outside the palpable terrestrial sequences of life. It began in this way. Returning one dark night from the store I became aware of the presence of a native at my side. It was the squatter Kapingy. He told me that he had a *shairi kubwa sana* – a very important matter to talk to me about. Putting out my lantern, so that my whereabouts should not be known, I walked with him to the bushes that grew on the hillock above the sheep-dip. I fancied at first he was going to give me some inside information about the stolen sheep. I was mistaken. He told me a long, rambling story concerning some mysterious man who had settled himself in the forest near the squatters' huts. All the time he was speaking he kept turning round as though he suspected the presence of eavesdroppers. The man, he explained, was all-powerful. He could, with a few grains of white dust, bring death to his enemies. He was feared by all. That very morning he had seized five fat goats belonging to Kapingy. Indeed there was no end to his exactions. I was furious. Who was this fellow who had had the audacity to plant himself down on the farm without so much as asking my leave? I would warm his jacket for him. 'Where is his hut?' I asked. 'You will find it,' replied Kapingy, 'if you follow the mud path that turns into the forest beyond the farther water-hole.'

The next morning found me on my pony riding along the track made by the bullock waggons when they hauled timber from the forest. A few hundred yards beyond the river, at the bottom of a dark overshadowed gully, I noticed the half-eaten carcass of a waterbuck which had evidently been killed the night before. I mention this fact because it seemed to me to have some relation to what happened afterwards. The ground all about was soiled and trampled upon.

By the time I had reached the boys' shamba the sun was high up above the escarpment. The clearing was radiant. Even during a drought it was pleasant to visit this place. It was always fresh and cool here, however hot it might be down on the plains. As soon as the boys became aware of my presence I was given a most friendly welcome. With bended backs they came crawling out of their cone-shaped huts like animals from their holes: men, women and tiny infants whose protruding bellies gave them the appearance of embryos born before their time and yet able to run about. I found the path that Kapingy had indicated. It very soon became so overgrown that I had to dismount. I had never explored this section of the forest before. The path eventually led to an open glen, in the centre of which stood the habitation of a witch-doctor. I knocked at the low door. There was no answer. I shouted, threatening to burn the place down unless its owner came out. Still there was no answer. Exasperated I took from my pocket a box of matches and set fire to the thatch. 'That,' I thought, 'will make the two-legged black rabbit bolt.' There was no fear of the fire spreading, as the glade was naked of grass, and with the utmost complacence I stood there watching the smoke curl upwards and upwards into the hot air. Suddenly I realized that a man was standing at my side. He was a middle-aged Kikuyu, but there was something about his demeanour and appearance that completely separated him from any native I had ever seen. He had an extremely cultured face, a face oddly reminding me of a certain portrait of Benjamin Disraeli which used to hang in the tap-room of the Choughs at Yeovil. It had the same sharp magpie look, the same black forelock. Feeling that I had behaved rather badly, I tried to restore myself by swearing. With a hundred oaths I asked him what the devil he was doing here in the forest. He replied with quiet dignity, and said if I would give him his sheep and goats he would depart that day. I was not to be placated. I drove him before me down the narrow path. He limped as he went, and I noticed that one of his feet was deformed.

As soon as we had reached the settlement I had all the sheep and goats driven into a single *boma* and set the squatters to the work of drafting them. I sat on my pony watching. Presently I noticed that one of the boys was laughing. I turned quickly and discovered that Kareba, the witch-doctor, was making the 'fig' at me, pointing at me with horned finger and thumb. It had evidently come to a struggle between their superstitious dread of the witch-doctor and my prestige as a white man. I turned my pony and rode after him, lashing at him with my whip. Lame as he was, the rogue was nimble, and, dodging behind trees, he managed to clamber on to a high rock well out of my way. I returned to the *boma*. But as I sat there looking at those lean, half-starved animals being dragged about by their owners I became more and more conscious of the concentrated gaze of this African priest, standing silent and alone upon his high pulpit rock. All that I had ever heard or read about spiritualism seemed more than plausible during that half-hour. I felt that he was computing the power of my unstable white soul, was focusing upon it a thousand maledictions. I forthwith determined to give him his goats without further molestation, but behold! when I had at last got them together he had gone, vanished into the forest. Immediately my heart hardened, and I gave instructions for the flock to be driven down to the homestead.

I was away all that day. When I returned towards evening the first things I saw were his grotesque bearded animals standing on tiptoe and trying to nibble at the small green leaves of a caper-tree. I was annoyed at being reminded of

197

the experiences of the morning and sent a message to the huts to say that if Kareba would come he could remove his possessions.

That evening after my supper had been cleared away I tried to read. It was out of the question. I was oppressed by a horrible sense of loneliness. What was I doing in this country, a white skin among so many black? The sultry wind of the dry season was sweeping across the Rift Valley. My wooden shutters rattled, the wattle-trees outside my window swayed backwards and forwards. A spirit of wild desolation had been let loose over the parched, vexed land. That evening I could well understand how certain settlers on out-of-the-way farms had drunk themselves to death. On such a night it was no pleasant thing to remember that I might well have an enemy abroad, an enemy out there in the gusty nightmare darkness. I went to bed early. I locked one of my doors; and the other, which stood opposite, I barricaded with a wire protection.

It must have been in the small hours of the morning, for the waning moon had risen, that I found myself wide awake, listening. It had not been a laugh that I had heard and it had not been a shriek, but it had seemed in its wavering undulations to have combined something of both. There it was again, long and loud, whining and wailing up from the forest, up from the gully, so I judged. I tried to reassure myself. Surely it was the howl of a hyena feasting on the remains of the dead buck. But even as my mind was suggesting this, my subconscious self knew well that it lied. That criminal human outcry could issue from no animal's throat! It had in it, so it seemed to my distraught fancy, all the tortured anguish, all the lunatic misery of the debased, outraged soul of the African negro. It was as if some insane inhabitant of the frightful continent had suddenly become articulate under the swinging frantic moon and had found himself impelled to give appalling utterance to all that his doomed race had suffered. Somewhere out there where the hispid branches swayed I knew there was a man with white canine teeth bared giving vent to BLACK LAUGHTER.

My nerves gave way. I could stand it no longer. I pressed my fingers to my ears. Unless my hands should be actually dragged from my head I should never listen to that sound again. A long time passed and still I lay on my back with my eyes closed. Then gradually I began to realize that the room had become filled with an extraordinary odour, an odour of putrefied blood and rotting flesh, *the odour of the breath of a hyena!* I sprang up. Not three yards away, drooping in my direction so that I could almost touch it, stood a motionless form. It was there and it was gone.

I slept no more that night. With my lantern burning at my bedside I waited for the morning. On going to the boys' huts to give them directions as to the day's work I asked them if they had heard anything in the night. 'Yes,' they said, ' the laughter of the man of God.' Still feeling uneasy I returned to my hut, entering by the door at which the thing had stood. It was broad daylight now, and there, stamped in the dust of the threshold, were two indents, one the footprint of a man, and the other the padded dog's spoor of an erect hyena. I knelt and examined them both closely. There was no mistake about it. The one foot was a foot with toes; the other a foot with claws!

CHAPTER TWENTY-FOUR
A Stockman's Hegira

*

ILL-OMENED indeed were the months succeeding this adventure. The drought never abated. The night winds grew hotter and hotter, and across a land blackened by fire, plague and fever ran wild. Each day conditions grew worse and yet no rain fell. Dysentery broke out, and many natives sickened and died. I would do what I could to look after them, but my efforts were to little purpose. The skin over their temples grew tight and dry. For a week or two they would lie about under the shrivelled bushes and then one morning when I called to them I would get no answer. It would now be my business to bury their bodies. I could expect no help on these occasions from the Kikuyu. Whenever they suspected the presence of death they would cower in their huts like so many pink-eyed pigeons who know that a sparrow-hawk is about. With only Asthmani, the old Swahili, to help me, I would have to lift the awkward unprotesting body on to a rude bier and carry it away. Each time we approached a fresh cadaver Asthmani would pluck some aromatic leaves and with quaint punctilious gravity stuff them up the two sunken nostrils. Upon reaching the grave we had prepared for our burden we would lay hold of the stiff-jointed subservient ankles and topple the corpse into the gaping aperture. Then alone I would return to my silent hut with hands smelling of mortality. It was like burying black cats; for what chance, what possible chance, I ask you, had these grimalkins of enjoying a blessed resurrection?

Rinderpest appeared amongst the cattle, and I would spend my days going from sick man to sick beast. With watering eyes and parched nostrils the herds would limp out to graze, with their despondent Masai behind them. Great funeral pyres could be seen in all directions and each of these smouldering bonfires of animal flesh was surrounded by hosts of marabou storks. The farm became infested with these melancholy birds. With bowed backs and bald heads they stalked to and fro, or settled motionless on the bare trees, or stood about, like a band of cowled Dominican monks, watching with half-closed exultant eyes the last few agonized moments of a sick bullock's life.

Rinderpest and dysentery! There was something horrible about the fact that these two diseases resembled one another so closely. One felt that the whole country – the tree stumps, the mould, the dry dusty tussocks – must be infected by the blood evacuated from the sick intestines of so many moribund men and so many moribund beasts.

And the devil was amongst the sheep also. On Saturdays when I took in the skins I found they were dying on an average of nearly a hundred a week. I would make post-mortem examinations, trying in vain to discover what was the matter with them. I would ignore the presence of the long slender tape-worms in their livers, the presence of countless wire-worms in their fourth stomachs, and come to the region of their lungs, which in every case I would find full of a yellow liquid. Heart water! That mysterious sickness became rampant. It was carried from one animal to another by ticks, which throughout that fatal season had burgeoned and thriven exceedingly.

It was now, when I was feeling completely fordone and at my wits' end, that my brother arrived. At last he had got his discharge. We went round the farm together. He looked at the

sheep, he looked at the countless skins pegged
out to dry round the camp-fires, and he looked at
the soiled, parched grazing grounds. 'When
stock are dying like this,' he said, 'it is time to
travel.' He suggested that we should migrate
with every sheep on the place to the unsurveyed
country on the other side of the Aberdare Mountains, where fresh pastures could still be found.
And I confess, when all arrangements had been
made, it was a mighty satisfaction to see the
flocks trailing toward the Thieves' Path with
their herders behind them and half-a-dozen
Kikuyu carriers bringing up the rear. My brother
and I followed a week later, he mounted on
Ramadan and I on Rosinante. We carried
ground-sheets and blankets under our saddles
and we also had bags of provisions hanging
down on both sides of our knees. We followed
the river till we reached the hot spring. Now
and then we would pass a watering-place where
the dusty ground had been made bare by the
treading of innumerable animals, by the treading
of sheep and cattle in the daytime, by the treading of zebra and buck in the evening, and by the
treading at night-time of all the various flesh-
eating creatures who require water as well as

blood to slake their thirst. At each of these openings we saw fragments of different kinds of animals who had sacrificed their lives in their desire for water; horns, ribs, and vertebræ were there, and also scraps of hide with hair still upon them, shrunken and twisted by the sun's heat. How sinister it was – these unfortunate infatuated herbivora, tormented by thirst to the point of madness, compelled to approach these treacherous banks! After we had left the hot spring we entered a deep valley which for some reason remained still unburnt. It was overgrown with tall elephant-grass, but we advanced easily, following a track made by buffalo. That night we slept with Fred Anderton. We were away early; indeed before ever the sun rose we had reached the edge of the great plain. The country here had the aspect of a vast desert, only instead of sand, miles upon miles of flat grassy stretches, the dry levels of which were broken by gigantic ant-hills, some of them twenty feet in circumference.

We rode and we rode, but as far as I could see drew no nearer to the mountains opposite. Our ponies became tired in the glaring heat and tripped against every tuft or stone that broke the uniform level. A lake appeared some few miles to our right and afterwards another in front of us. This was disconcerting, as the natives had led us to suppose that the waters of Lake El Bordossat lay farther to the north. 'We may be able to find some way round,' I said, and we rode on. But after moving forward for another half-hour the lakes before us seemed no nearer than the mountains. One got the impression of being in some nightmare dreamland where one could go on for ever without arriving at any destination. And then we saw an extraordinary thing occur. A herd of zebra, startled at our approach, galloped under the trees surrounding the lake opposite us straight into the water. On and on they went without a single splash rising from the glittering frozen surface. We understood at last. The lake was a mirage, was one of those insubstantial phantoms which by their visible reality make one suspect that the very world itself is but a dream outside a dream.

We continued our journey, the sun beating down upon us and upon our ponies. Would we ever get across those sweltering leagues? When I put my hand on Rosinante's neck I found it moist with sweat. Forward we went. On every

side of us now countless El Bordossats glim-
mered and twinkled. We could see the lakes
perfectly clearly, with deceptive rushes and
false broad-leafed palm-trees growing on their
shores.

We now approached the Milowa river, which,
with a hundred bends, meanders across this
wilderness. As we came down the last slope my
horse's hoof clicked against something in the
grass. My brother dismounted and picked up
the jawbone of a lion! We decided to off-saddle
at the ford.

We were within a few yards of it when, looking in to a kind of ditch-like place, we saw
the body of a native lying head downwards, with
stiff beaded legs protruding grotesquely against
the side of the bank. We passed on. I was in
two minds to go back and discover what had
killed the man in this out-of-the-way place, but
then I remembered I was in Africa. After all it
was none of my business. A dead nigger more
or less, what did it matter?

We continued our journey. Once more we
were crossing the plain. Our interest was now
arrested by a white object in front of us. From
the distance it looked like a Somali standing

207

motionless in his spotless linen garment. We
drew nearer. It was the bleached skull of an
elephant! The monotony of this part of our
ride was relieved by the presence of a leopard
which had evidently been delayed in its return
from its midnight hunting. We followed it. A
Thomson's gazelle was scampering about it, now
in front, now behind, as if it wanted to attract
the animal's attention. We imagined that it must
have had a young one hidden not far off and was
displaying the same maternal anxiety that a nest-
ing bird will sometimes show when it thinks the
safety of its offspring is threatened. Whenever
we came up close, the leopard would break into
a run. For some reason it looked almost black,
perhaps because we were never near enough to
see the spots on its pelt. It reached the shelter of
the forested slopes a few minutes before we did.
It took us nearly three hours to reach the top of
the Aberdare range. We had to lead our ponies
most of the way. Once on the summit of the
mountains we were rewarded by a splendid view
of the great primeval forest extending eastward,
fold upon fold of wooded hills, as yet practically
unknown to the white man, inhabited only by
Wandorobos, that most primitive of all the

African peoples, who gain a precarious existence by entangling the feet of wild animals with the creepers which hang from the trees. We soon found a good camping place, and after a refreshing bath in a cold stream lay down in the shade, soothed by that feeling of utter solitude which in the wilderness falls upon the soul like a benediction. The night was wonderful. With indifferent unconscious solemnity the constellations rose one after the other into their places, leaving us sleeping there amid strange mutterings.

We were up early and had crossed several miles of rolling downlands before the dawn. There were no trees here, simply grass-grown hills rising one behind the other. When we came to the place where the descent began and the forest once more encroached upon the bare hills we rested. After we had talked for some time sitting under a tree, the roots of which spread themselves into the ground like the tentacles of an octopus, we noticed that the branches above us were covered with stones. We both understood the meaning of this. The natives who passed this way considered the path down which we were going to be extremely dangerous. It is a custom with them when they are about to embark upon any perilous track to place stones on trees in this way. It is, I take it, a superstition akin to our practice of touching wood in order to forestall any shrewd turn that destiny may have in store for us. I regarded these votive offerings with interest and no little apprehension. Some still adhered to the flat branches like barnacles, but others had fallen to the ground and lay in heaps near the spot where we were sitting. The wind perhaps had blown them down. Certainly no native would have had the courage to displace them. Some of these stones may have lain here for more than a hundred years, stones that had originally been put into place by black fingers which had long ago crumbled to dust, had been put into place perhaps on the very afternoon that Shelley was drowned, or when William Cowper set out for Norfolk with my great-grandfather. There was something alarming about that descent through the forest. Huge trees, as high almost as the redwoods which grow at the foot of Mount Tamalpais in California, entirely shut out the sunlight, and as our ponies slid step by step through the rank foliage it was easy to imagine how muffled would be the cry of any wretch overtaken by evil in such a place. Once out on the open veldt our advance was more rapid. We had still some twenty miles to cover before reaching our camp on the banks of the Guaso Nyiro river. On this side of the mountains it seemed hotter than ever; half dozing in our saddles we rode on and on. Even when the sun had sunk low in the heavens the air seemed to retain the stifling heat of noon. There was plenty of grass about albeit grey as a badger's back. Herds of zebra, eland, kongoni were grazing everywhere. Suddenly coming over the rise of a hill we found ourselves in full sight of Mount Kenya. I shall never forget that moment. It was amazing to raise one's eyes from the hot lowlands and find them resting upon the snow-fields and glacial slopes of this towering, peaked mountain, over the white crest of which the Equator actually passes.

Presently we came upon some of the sheep, the wethers which had been camped above the great rock. We stopped and talked to the Masai herder. He told us that the sheep were no longer dying. Following his directions we made our way towards a clump of thorn-trees where he said our tent had been pitched. That night as we feasted upon a guinea-fowl well basted with

goat's fat an infinite sense of contentment de-
scended upon us. Had we not put nearly one
hundred miles between us and those churlish
marabou storks?

CHAPTER TWENTY-FIVE
On the Banks of the Guaso Nyiro

*

THOSE months I spent with my brother on the banks of the Guaso Nyiro were happy. The war had come to an end and I knew that in a little time I should be journeying down to the coast in order to set sail for England. At last the responsibility of looking after the sheep had fallen from my shoulders. They might get foot-rot, get scabby, die by the thousand; from henceforth it was nothing to me.

Our tent was pitched under a group of trees which stood on the top of a slope some two hundred yards from the river. We spent our days riding over the great plains, across which, night and morning, the pointed shadow of Mount Kenya fell. I saw an oryx for the first time, that peculiar antelope whose horns are as sharp as rapiers, and which many believe to be the original unicorn. Sometimes we would come upon a rhinoceros out in the open and would follow it for several miles as it went lumbering forward. My dog, Egypt, would rush in at it, and the great beast would snort and charge. I

would carefully note the distance which separated
it from me and if I did not consider the space
wide enough would turn my horse's head and
ride in the opposite direction. Towards evening
we would walk to the top of a hill and sit under
a certain stunted thorn-tree which had three
twisted branches, and watch the red glow on the
heights of Mount Kenya fade slowly into grey.
After supper we would go into our tent and lie
down, and the light from our lantern would
illuminate the pale interior, revealing the fact
that a hundred flies, ordinary house flies, had
settled upon the canvas ceiling above our heads
in soporific trance. And lying there side by side
under that slight canopy, which itself was enclosed by the enormous canopy of the night sky
outside, my brother would take his flute from a
a pocket in the side of the tent and begin to play
the 'Kingsbury jig', or some other West-country
ditty familiar to us both, and capable of filling
our drowsy heads with memories of far-off village festivals in shady orchards on the banks of
the River Parret. We would see it all as clearly
as if we had never left the ancient shire – the
uniformed bandsmen with dusty boots leading
forward the straggling village revellers, the ban-

ners, the flags, the girls in white frocks, the delicate hems of which were so soon to be stained with green grass sap.

And then we would go to sleep, and if ever one opened one's eyes during those long black hours it was to realize that the whole country beyond the river and out and away towards Kenya was resonant with the voices of lions. Looking out through the lancet opening of the tent door, beyond where the ponies stood tethered, one could almost fancy one saw the great tawny heads lowered as the last subsiding grunts shook the air. We would wake early and wash in a bucket of chill water brought up by Kamoha from the river, and as we stood snuffing in the fresh tropical air the purple wooded slopes of the mountains opposite would grow more and more defined.

One night we were awakened by a most diabolical uproar. My brother jumped out of bed and snatched up his rifle. The sound came from somewhere behind our tent. The boys crept from their grass huts, scared out of their wits. My brother did his best to steady the ponies, which were trying to break away. The sound continued for several minutes, roar upon roar of mad ferocity, and then stopped as abruptly as it had begun. We both felt convinced that lions alone were capable of making such a din. But what could they have been killing? The morning solved the problem. We found a dead lion not two hundred yards away. It was very large and in perfect condition, but its body had been terribly mangled. It looked as though it had been hacked to death with a hatchet. In the dust leading away from where it lay were the footprints of a second lion – footprints, *sasa tembo* ('like an elephant's'), as Kamoha said, and indeed they were enormous. What an encounter it must have been, lion and super-lion wrestling together amongst the thorns! Who could have withstood the pulse-beats of their infuriated hearts, the strength of their contorted muscles, the red flash of their yellow-lidded eyes as they revolved to and fro in a fatal embrace under the star-shine of the Southern Cross? Now that I am once more living in civilized surroundings I come to appreciate how liberating to my spirit the mere contemplation of such African incidents has been. When I am in danger of being encaged in this or that cleverly baited bourgeois trap I have but to think of that sublime battle, and petty considerations, petty preoccupations, fall into place. We kept a lean nanny-goat during this time and used to depend upon her for our milk. We breakfasted under some trees a few yards from the tent. We had made a kind of arbour there, and very pleasant it was to eat porridge in this shaded retreat where no flies came. I soon grew to like goat's milk, and whenever during the day my eye fell upon the lanky creature I would send a boy to milk her. Also, I am ashamed to say, when night fell we would as often as not use her for bait in the box trap we had made for leopards. One night I discovered Kamoha giving some of this thrice precious milk to a strange boy who was eating posho near the fire. I stopped and talked for a few moments. Our visitor was a Kikuyu and it turned out had been the companion of the dead native we had passed near the Milowa river. Thus quite accidentally I came to hear what had taken place. The Kikuyus apparently had been camping near the ford when they saw three Somali traders approaching on mules. After their fashion they hid in the bushes and watched. At midnight, when they judged by the silence and the lowness of the fire that the traders were asleep, they crept out in the hope of being able to steal a bag of rice which was resting against one of the saddles. The murdered boy had ventured nearest, only to feel his ankle suddenly held fast. At the first sound of his terrified wailing his companion, with whom I was now talking, had fled away into the tangled growths of the river bank. Meanwhile the Somali, without a moment's thought, had unsheathed his ornamented knife and slit open the thief's navel as though he had been a jumping hare. He then put some more logs on to the fire and once more curled up to sleep. The narrator concluded his story by simply remarking, 'There is no fooling with Somalis.' He then went on eating his pottage as though it was all past history. 'Certainly,' I thought, as I entered the tent, 'this is a land for the living. People have short memories in Africa for dead men.'

At last the day came for me to set out on my return journey over the Aberdare Mountains. I was to stay for a few days in the Rift Valley and then travel down to the coast to wait there for a ship to take me to England. My brother rode a day's journey with me. Tired out after our long trek we at last reached the Sugeroi river, where we intended to spend the night. We had thought of camping actually at the ford, but we found that it was evidently used as a drinking place by all the forest animals. We decided therefore to cross and look for a more suitable position farther along the river bank. Soon we came upon exactly what we wanted, an open space of ground by a dead fallen tree. We off-saddled and collected wood for our fire. We filled our saucepan with water from the river, made a tent out of a ground-sheet, and cut grass for the ponies. We half-expected to have trouble that night, but we were too tired to take any precautions beyond heaping our fire with logs and placing our guns ready to hand. As a matter of fact we slept till dawn. We breakfasted on rice and tea. We were just finishing our meal when, ringing across from the forest, came the shrill trumpeting of elephants. They were obviously coming down our way. We got our things together, raised our camp, said farewell, and parted.

After I had ridden a little distance I looked back. From where I was I could clearly see the dead tree, the smoke of our fire, and my brother's figure receding and receding over the veldt. Suddenly, as I stood watching, five elephants emerged from the forest and began moving over the very place where our camp had been. They must have avoided the smouldering fire, because early in this year, 1924, I received a letter from my brother saying that he had passed by the Sugeroi river and found the place of our camp still undisturbed. The three stones upon which we had balanced our saucepan were as we had left them, and beneath a tangled mat of grass he had actually discovered some charred ends of the sticks that had been burned by us on the eve of St. Mark, 1919.

CHAPTER TWENTY-SIX

Blood! Blood! Blood!

*

I REACHED the Rift Valley to find it completely transformed. Rain had fallen, and the plains and craters and forest slopes were once more covered with fresh green grass. The feathered rushes of the lake's margin once more stood swaying in deep water. I stayed there for two weeks, wandering over the familiar ground of my past labours like a revenant. Marvellous indeed was the sensation of freedom I experienced!

The day before I left I went down to the shore of Lake Elmenteita. The sheepman's diary that I used for my counts was in my pocket and I determined if possible to catch in a single piece of prose something of the dark mood of the country. In those days I used to wear a glaring red shirt. At noon I took off my coat and continued to write with this gay garment exposed. Presently I realized that the sky above my head was darkened. The vultures had come down. They had seen something red lying still and that could mean only one thing to them – BLOOD! BLOOD! BLOOD! It was a happening truly in accord with the manner of the continent. And from its socket of infinite space the abnormal yellow eye of the tropical sun continued with malicious aplomb to stare down upon that host of hooped godless fowls encircling the fugitive figure of a renegade stockman who, go where he might, was destined to carry upon his back till the day of his death the shocking striped brand of Africa.